TRAVELS THROUGH DALI

DALI

with a leg of ham

ZHANG MEI

To my father, Zhang Minqiang,
who taught me everything about Yunnan.
In memory of my mother, Liu Rongzhen,
who rests on the Cangshan Mountains.

CONTENTS

PREFACE

ODE TO A HAM

Ham: The hind leg of a pig above the hock joint, cut from the carcass and cured by salting and drying, and sometimes smoking, so that it will keep for months at room temperature.
The Oxford Companion to Food

THE SWEET, nutty aroma of sizzling ham always signalled a good meal.

As a little girl growing up in Dali, I would peer into the wok, watching my father stir-fry a little ham fat before adding the lean pieces along with a big bowlful of crunchy garlic scapes or spicy green peppers and onions. At the table, my brothers and I would burrow into the dish with our chopsticks, eager to fish out little ruby jewels of hammy goodness among the vegetables. They were always faster with their chopsticks, but I always won the last piece of ham. I was the only girl sandwiched between two boys, so all I needed to do was cry 'unfair!' and my father would stare them down and let me take my pick.

Ham was expensive, though, so we didn't eat it very often. In the mid 1970s in China, rationing was still in full swing. A pound of meat had to last our household a month. My father would always choose a fatty chunk of pork because it produced more lard, which for us had absolutely no association with cholesterol. Half a teaspoon of lard, soy sauce, salt, spring onion – add hot water and you've got the base for a bowl of delicious noodle soup.

Dali was a beautiful town to grow up in, cradled between the soaring Cangshan Mountains, strewn with fields of wild flowers, and the glassy Erhai Lake. I wondered back then what life was like beyond those mountains of Dali, beyond Kunming, the provincial capital, and Yunnan.

When I left for graduate school in the US, as far as I knew, Yunnan was the only place on earth that produced ham. Of course, when I walked into the Kresge Dining Hall of Harvard Business School and encountered a ham and cheese sandwich, I realised that was not the case. But the dining hall ham tasted nothing like the ham I knew and loved; after that sandwich, I was convinced Yunnan was the only place on earth that produced tasty ham.

My life took on a different trajectory after I graduated, and the flavour of Yunnan ham faded in my memory. That is, until one Thanksgiving, when an entire leg of ham turned up in the mail at my house in Maryland, a gift from my American father-in-law. This ham was different. It was smoked and ready to eat as soon as you produced a sharp knife to carve off a slice. And it tasted really good. What sort of ham was this, I inquired eagerly? Virginia ham!

Wow, this is almost as good as Yunnan ham, I thought. But ham in America was served differently, carved into big slices and dished up on a platter at our Thanksgiving table. We ate merrily for one night, then stared at the three-quarters of a leg occupying a whole shelf in our refrigerator, wondering how many more ham sandwiches we could consume before it went bad or we went mad.

I made up my mind – no more ham sandwiches for me. That remaining leg of ham was sliced up, julienned or diced, then fried with rice, garlic shoots, broccoli, green chilli, spring onion, or practically anything else I could find in the refrigerator. No additional seasoning was needed. Tastes and aromas from years before came flooding back to me.

Later, I was introduced to Italian prosciutto, Spanish *jamón ibérico* – all these different hammy delicacies celebrated across the world. The more I travelled, the more similarities presented themselves, even among vastly different cultures. When I drove around the small villages in Spain, I knew immediately why they would cure ham, as the climate and sunshine felt just like Dali. Humans separated by continents had come up with the same solutions to cure meat; cultural gaps were filled by something as simple as a leg of ham.

Yet, when I tell people about Yunnan ham, the first response is often, Really? Yunnan produces ham? Most people outside the country, even outside of Yunnan, have no idea.

In the year 2000, I founded WildChina, a travel company, with the aim of connecting travellers from around the world with the disappearing traditions of China. From my perch in Beijing I began to see Yunnan and Dali through different eyes. Their beauty and importance jumped out at me, moving me in ways they never had before. I felt an urgent need to share the stories of my childhood – the traditions, history and way of life that were so normal to me growing up, but are already alien for my children. That's where this book comes in.

Just as a few chunks of salty Yunnan ham can make a dish come alive, so, I figured, that same ham can be a catalyst in other ways. For me, the most joyful by-product of food and eating is people coming together to share stories.

So why not go to Dali, find a leg of ham, and do what I do best – travel, share it with friends, and find some stories and recipes from a part of the world I feel privileged to call home.

Zhang Mei
2016

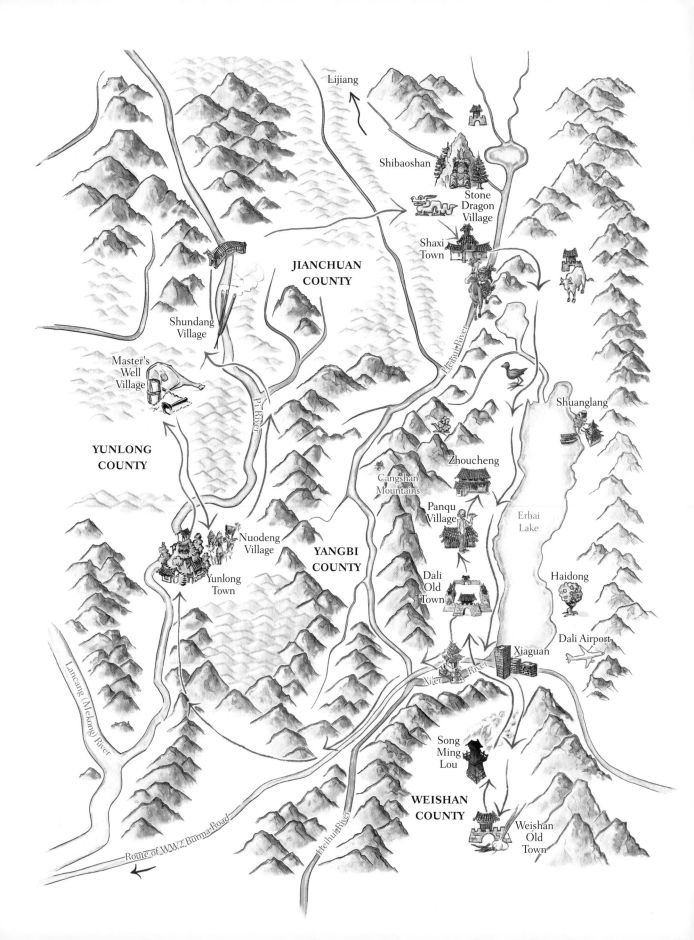

INTRODUCTION

THE FOUNDING story of Dali is often passed down orally from generation to generation. This is the way my uncle told the story to me.

On 25 June in the year 737, a king named Pi Luo Ge invited five other rulers from neighbouring dominions around Erhai Lake to come together and pay their respects to the gods.

The wife of one of these rulers, Queen Bai Jie, didn't like the sound of the invitation her husband had received. She had never cared for Pi Luo Ge – his aggressive manner and the way he looked at her. She begged her husband not to go, but he didn't dare slight the king by rejecting his invitation. So, for good luck, Queen Bai Jie put an iron bracelet on her husband's wrist.

Pi Luo Ge had built a shiny new palace called Song Ming Lou, and that was where all the rulers gathered. A magnificent banquet went on and on, with dancing and partying late into the night. At one point, Pi Luo Ge left the building to take care of some business, and it was then that a fire broke out; soon, helped by the wind, it engulfed Song Ming Lou in a raging inferno.

On hearing the news, Queen Bai Jie mounted her horse, torch in hand, and galloped off to rescue her husband. But by the time she had made the 60-kilometre journey through the mountains, Song Ming Lou was a smoking ghost, with barely a frame of timber left standing. She clawed through the pile of charred debris until her fingers were bleeding, and she eventually found the remains of her husband, identifiable only by the iron bracelet.

Seizing the opportunity, Pi Luo Ge proposed to the newly widowed Bai Jie; he had long been an admirer of her beauty and intelligence. She agreed on the condition that he grant her a hundred-day period of mourning for her husband. On the hundredth day, she went to Erhai Lake to commemorate her husband one final time, and drowned herself in the water.

Having destroyed all his competitors in the fire, Pi Luo Ge took over the five neighbouring kingdoms. So it was that a group of warrior kingdoms were united in fire, blood, treachery and suicide. The result was the Kingdom of Nanzhao (and later the Kingdom of Dali), with Pi Luo Ge as the first of many kings. At the height of its power, Nanzhao stretched across Yunnan and into Sichuan, Tibet, Myanmar and Laos; it allied itself with China's incumbent Tang and later Song Dynasties.

The heart of the kingdom that Pi Luo Ge so coveted was a fertile belt of gently sloping land 40 kilometres long and just a few kilometres wide, sandwiched between the impenetrable walls of the Cangshan Mountains to the west and the sea-like expanse of Erhai Lake to the east.

It was a natural stronghold, tapering in the north and south into defensible passes. A perfect, resource-rich, secure realm.

Dali.

Over 1000 years later, this land remains the heart of Dali Bai Autonomous Prefecture, and its present-day population of Bai and Yi people are spiritual heirs to those kingdoms from long ago.

Dali is nestled in a quiet corner of Yunnan Province. The most southwesterly of China's thirty-four provinces, Yunnan literally means 'south of the clouds', so named for its position on a southern shelf of the Tibetan massif. I've always thought it a suitably romantic title for a place that lays claim to some of the richest ecology on Earth.

Yunnan has long represented the final frontier of the Chinese empire, historically sheltered from the rest of the country by the craggy mountain ranges of Sichuan Province to the north, and Guizhou and Guangxi provinces to the east. Kunming, a city of over 3 million people, is over 2000 kilometres from Beijing. Kunming is closer to Yangon in Myanmar to the west, and Vientiane or Hanoi to the south.

Yunnan is also one of China's most ethnically diverse provinces, with upward of twenty-five different non-Han ethnic groups. The Dali valley is mostly populated with Bai people, who have blended Chinese and other Asian customs into their own traditions, reflected in the highly localised version of the Bon religion, distinct from Tibetan Bon worship, Chinese Buddhism and Taoism.

As heirs to the Kingdom of Dali, the Bai settled the fertile plains

between the Cangshan Mountains and Erhai Lake. Plains in Yunnan are called *bazi* (坝子), and Dali *bazi*, watered by the streams flowing off the Cangshan Mountains, are some of the most fertile lands of all.

But Dali is also home to sizable Yi and Hui populations. The Yi built most of their communities in the mountains, and the Hui – who generally practice Islam – clustered together in another *bazi*, Weishan, to the south of Dali.

Dali's temperate climate has always lent itself to human settlement. The days are warm and sun-drenched while the nights are cool and refreshing. There's neither a bitter cold winter nor a scorching hot summer. Fruit, vegetables and rice grow easily in the rich soil, bright sunshine and crisp air. These conditions also mean cured meats last for years without going bad.

Dali especially has long held an irresistible allure for outsiders. The region was once a thriving trade centre along the ancient Tea and Horse Caravan Road, which transferred bricks of tea produced in the Pu'er region of southern Yunnan all the way north into Tibet, where tea was almost as essential an everyday item as salt. Many Dali traders operated caravans in treacherous conditions through regions plagued by bandits or disease. The return on such ventures was significant, as evidenced by the many architecturally stunning ancient wooden homes that still dot small villages throughout the mountains.

In the nineteenth century, Western missionaries were lured into the region in search of rare rhododendrons and azaleas. By 1910, the French had built a narrow-gauge railway connecting their colonial dominion of Indochina with the sunny environs of Kunming (for comparison, the railway from Kunming to Chengdu in Sichuan Province wasn't completed until 1970). The French brought Catholicism, too, converting a few communities of Tibetans in Yunnan who still practice that faith to this day.

In the 1920s and 1930s, Western adventurers were also drawn to the area. Yunnan is generally believed to be the setting for James Hilton's novel *Lost Horizon*, about a harmonious, monastic land named Shangri-La where no one ever grows old. In the 1980s and 1990s, another generation of explorers made their way to Dali, tempted by banana pancakes, good coffee and the marijuana that grows wild throughout the valley.

Even more recently, Dali has become a destination for well-heeled Chinese (and the occasional foreigner) fleeing the hustle and bustle of urban China. They are known as *Xin Dali Ren* (new Dali folk). Artists, editors and photographers, they choose Dali over the competitive rat race in major cities. In that way, Dali remains a kind of frontier that can still feel a long way from anywhere. 'Heaven is high and the emperor is far away,' as the old Chinese saying goes.

The name Dali (Ta-Li in older books) is used today to refer to three different entities:

Dali Bai Autonomous Prefecture (*Dali Zhou*)

An area the size of Belgium, Dali is one of Yunnan's sixteen prefectures. The Cangshan Mountains anchor the prefecture in the middle, and Kunming lies to the east.

Dali Old Town (*Dali Gucheng*)

This beautiful walled town and tourist hotspot, about 1 kilometre wide and 2 kilometres long, is what people typically mean when they talk about 'going to Dali' as a visitor or tourist. It sits between the Cangshan Mountains and Erhai Lake, and is surrounded by waves of white-walled villages and acres of farmland cascading down to the lakeshore.

New Dali City (*Xin Dali Shi* or, traditionally, Xiaguan)

Twelve kilometres to the south of Dali Old Town, the modern city of Xiaguan is the official capital of Dali Prefecture. This is where government entities sit – the prefecture governor, the court, etc.

Our journey begins from my home in Dali Old Town. A few years ago, I bought a place close to the south gate of the old city wall, with views over sloping rooftops toward the lake. My husband and I bring the kids here from Beijing for Chinese New Year, to watch fireworks explode over the lake, ride bicycles and hike among the tea plantations on the Cangshan Mountains. But the trip I planned this time would be different.

Travelling by road, we set off for a week-long sojourn through the region. There are four of us: photographer Liz, creative director Tom, my younger brother Zhang Ye at the wheel, and me.

From Dali Old Town, we drive southwest across the Cangshan Mountains to the neighbouring county of Yunlong, a little-visited place famous for its salt and ham. That is where we pick up our leg of ham.

From Yunlong we head north into Jianchuan County and Shaxi, and finally down south to the land of Pi Luo Ge and present day Weishan, before doubling back to Dali Old Town. It's a loop that takes us past bustling towns as well as far-flung villages, some of which I visited long ago, and some of which I've never set foot in. We embark on a quest of delicious discovery that starts with a leg of ham.

YUNLONG COUNTY

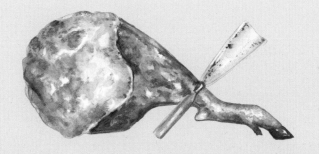

SALT AND HAM

THE FIRST task before us is to secure a locally cured leg of ham. We head south from the gates of Dali Old Town past Xiaguan, then westward along the precipitous banks of the Xi'er River. The highway, tracing the old Burma Road, will eventually reach Myanmar. That's how the highway goes, and anything deviating too far from it is somewhat forgotten. Yunlong, our ham country, veers far off the highway.

People in Yunnan have the habit of connecting a place with a product. Want walnuts? Go to Yangbi. Pears? Haidong. And ham? Xuanwei in northeast Yunnan, although Xuanwei's production has mostly relocated from villages to factories now.

For our ham, we will be travelling to Yunlong to find the smallholder pastoral ham. Only Dali locals know about Yunlong ham. Unlike the Bai who farm and fish in Erhai Valley around Dali Old Town, the Bai of Yunlong have perfected the art of ham curing. They enjoy the advantage of essential ham-curing conditions: a dry mountain climate and an abundance of locally produced salt.

It's late March when we embark on our ham quest, already deep into spring in this part of the country. Peach, apple and pear trees are in bloom, dotting the fields of green with red, pink and white. Spring is a particularly beautiful time here, with mild temperatures in the low 20s Celsius during the day, and just a little chill at night. People have returned home after Chinese New Year, so we have a better chance of finding them back at their routines.

About an hour out of Xiaguan, we take a turn north. The road narrows to one lane on each side and winds along a small river. The water in the river is clear. Mountains rise sharply on both sides of the road, with very little open space for panoramic views.

A sign proclaims that we are entering Yunlong County. More than three-quarters of Yunlong's population is Bai, scattered like seeds over a swathe of green-carpeted mountains and forested valleys. Eighteen other ethnic groups live here too, including the Lisu, Yi, Miao, Hui and even a group closely related to the Thai.

The mountains have historically made transportation and communication difficult, which is why residents of Yunlong produce everything locally, growing vegetables and grains, harvesting produce in season, and herding animals on the nearby mountains. They also produce the essential ingredient in ham production: salt.

Yes, salt. We eat too much of it, but it is also essential for human survival. All over the world, the humble compound has been a precious resource, over which wars have been fought and great power amassed.

In fact, salt, a plain commodity, has an illustrious history in China. In his book *Salt: A World History*, Mark Kurlansky describes how salt revenue was used to build the Great Wall and raise armies. In the Tang Dynasty (618–907), half the revenue of the Chinese state was derived from salt. Even earlier, in the third century BC, Li Bing, an administrator of the Qin Dynasty, ordered the drilling of the world's first salt wells.

Yunlong is home to several such salt wells; at its peak during the Ming Dynasty in the fourteenth century, there were eight famous salt wells operating in the area. Five were clustered around Yunlong town, and their salt – collectively known as Five Well Salt – was a premium brand, sold throughout western Yunnan and all the way to Myanmar.

After successive dynasties of prosperity, Yunlong's salt economy collapsed in 1949 when the government reorganised the salt trade. The merchants departed their grand houses in the salt villages, and the ancient trade ceased.

The fact that Yunlong was once a main salt centre of Yunnan is no longer highlighted in any government brochure. At least, that was the case until a small village called Nuodeng was featured in a documentary series called *A Bite of China*, which aired on national TV in 2012. Since then, Yunlong has been making its way back on to the map, luring travellers eager to learn more about the county's artisanal salt and ham.

In Yunlong town, an old friend, Mr Zhang Jiahong, is waiting for us in the yellowing light of late afternoon. He's a Yunlong native on good terms with villagers all over the county – a perfect fixer for our ham and salt quest. 'I'll meet you here at 7:30 in the morning,' he says solemnly. 'Don't be late.'

THE SALT MAKING OF
MASTER'S WELL VILLAGE

WE FOLLOW the road north along Bi River, which the locals call Pi River, as it meanders past white-walled Bai villages. Elegant, covered wooden bridges every few kilometres are a fading monument to the historic salt wealth of the region. This indicates that we are close to our first destination, Master's Well Village.

It's just before noon when we arrive, and Mr Yang Zhiguang, a salt maker, is waiting for us on a dusty, unpaved road leading up to the village. He smiles grandly from behind a silvery moustache and guides us past school children and ragged ponies hauling building materials on their tawny backs.

Salt Maker Yang leads us on a short walk to his production area, the only one in the village. Here, salt is still extracted from a well and crystallised, using a traditional process unchanged for centuries. Under a makeshift shelter we find a trio of enormous black iron woks (you could easily cook an entire pig in one of them), bubbling and frothing like witches' cauldrons. Brine is being pumped from a well below so it can be boiled with the scorching, steady heat of tree trunk-sized logs stuffed inside clay kilns beneath the woks.

A worker in a stained grey vest uses a large ladle to spoon rough hunks of crystallising rock salt out of the water and into a bamboo strainer. Flies congregate woozily in the acrid, stuffy air. The well is only 5 metres deep, or maybe 10 – the old man at the woks isn't sure. From the outside it's little more than a rough hole in the ground. Aside from the mechanical pump, this is a process that hasn't changed for hundreds of years.

It's a relief to leave the fumes of the salt well and breathe the cool air of the village once again. Salt Maker Yang guides us nimbly up narrow mud paths that rise between homesteads. Every so often we step aside to let horses pass, obedient to the orders of the young men on their backs. A lady greets us, carrying her daughter's baby in a wicker crib that hangs from a strip of cloth around her shoulders.

Yang's house is perched near the top of the village. This is where, in the open air of their concrete porch, he and his wife process the salt further and prepare it for market. On a table, salt cakes are drying in uniform rows of off-white cylinders that

taper at one end. Each is around a kilogram (*2 jin*) in weight.

Salt Maker Yang places a big heap of raw salt into a wooden mortar and bashes it repeatedly to make the grains finer. The salt is then pressed evenly into a wooden mould, which is held by its handle and rotated like a Tibetan monk's prayer wheel – tapped gently as it turns – to form a neat shape and loosen the salt from the mould. Finally, the mould is gently removed and the edges are cleaned with a knife. The salt cake dries in the open air for two days, during which time its colour fades.

The process then moves to Yang's wife, who employs rice straw to tie two salt cylinders together, back to back, yielding a beautiful plat that also serves to protect the salt's surface during transportation. It's a deft, artistic handicraft, and the end result looks lovely. I marvel to think that salt has been produced and packaged in this way, in these parts, for hundreds if not thousands of years.

Traditionally, Five Well Salt is produced in blocks of 2 to 3 *jin*, 7 to 8 *jin*, or, at its largest, 10 *jin*. Salt can be shaped into drums, traditional scale weights, lanterns or even cute laughing Buddhas or lions. Villagers like those in Master's Well prefer the 10-*jin* cakes, as they last longer. Salt Maker Yang's smaller 2-*jin* cakes are geared more toward the emerging tourist market.

Table salt is processed with an anti-caking agent to make it tumble willingly out of a shaker. Master's Well salt is unadorned, and its caking qualities help it adhere to hams. It is naturally rich in potassium but lacks iodine, which is added to commercially produced salt. This means that when locals salt their hams, they use a fifty-fifty mix, Yang explains.

According to Zhang, local salt, referred to as *tu yan*(土盐), offers a slightly sweeter aftertaste, as opposed to the more bitter aftertaste of commercial table salt. Locals prefer *tu yan* for salting ham or pickling vegetables, and occasionally animal feed. The white salt cakes have a hint of dirt-yellow to them, and *tu yan* crystals are finer.

The salt cakes tell the story of the commodity's transportation. Salt was traditionally traded, along with tea, on the Tea and Horse Caravan Road. Like the salt cakes, tea from Pu'er was steamed and compressed into transportable puck-shaped discs or bricks. Centuries ago, salt from Master's Well Village would have made the long journey over snow-clogged passes and barren plateaus to be traded for the region's hardy Tibetan ponies.

Salt Maker Yang sells me a pair of salt cakes. He carefully packs them in a paper box, cushioning them with more rice straw and carrying the box back down the hill for us, leading the way to a neighbouring family who will help us cure our ham.

THE HAM CURING OF
MASTER'S WELL VILLAGE

'THIS IS the guy. He has your ham,' Zhang tells us, motioning to Mr Yang Xuegong.

Yang, as you will find out, is a family name shared by many Bai people in Dali prefecture. This Yang, a farmer, has silvery sideburns framing a lively face darkened by fifty-nine summers in sub-alpine conditions.

Zhang grins enthusiastically and doles out cigarettes to Farmer Yang and one of his sons. Yang and his wife have three sons all together, in addition to one daughter and two grandchildren, all of whom live in this village.

Farmer Yang smiles shyly as we loiter in the yard of his farmhouse, which is on a hillside in the valley. In the yard is a clutter of tools, motorcycle parts, clucking chickens and children's toys, all cloaked in mingling aromas of wood smoke, cow dung and freshly brewed tea. Mushrooms dry in garland-like necklaces, hanging on nails tacked into the wood-panelled wall. A small handheld wooden loom gathers dust in the corner. Beside it sits a neat pair of cloth shoes whose cotton soles are stitched with thick knots, similar to those found on the feet of the terracotta warriors.

As if on cue, another of Yang's sons enters the yard, brandishing an enormous haunch of pink flesh like a club. The Yangs no longer raise their own pigs, having switched to chicken farming some years ago. Our ham-to-be, weighing in at a hefty 26 *jin* (13 kilograms), is sourced from the local market.

A table is cleared and the leg plopped, fat side up, on to it. There is a hush; all eyes turn to Farmer Yang as he takes a chopstick, breaks it lengthwise to create a spear-like point, and pierces the blotchy flesh in a dozen places to help the salt penetrate. His granddaughter, a 5-year-old in a peach top, clings shyly to the leg of her uncle. It's a ritual they've all watched before.

Farmer Yang washes his hands and unscrews an old water bottle. 'Corn alcohol,' he says, massaging the sweet-smelling liquor into the flesh. The alcohol, while killing off bacteria, will work as an adhesive for the salt. 'And it gives the ham a sweeter taste,' adds Zhang, nodding knowingly.

I pass one of my cylinders of Master's Well salt to Yang. He crumbles it like a sandcastle, adds some store-bought salt, and pats the mix liberally on to the ham, the

plump meat cushioning under his slow, steady touch. Eventually the leg is entirely shrouded in what looks like half an inch of day-old snow. It's a mesmerising ritual: Farmer Yang, cigarette dangling from his lips, raises the ham-to-be by the ankle and affectionately works salt into every nook and cranny.

Satisfied, he takes a sip of tea and proceeds to explain how a heavy stone will be positioned on top of the leg to squeeze out the moisture, which is then collected and boiled to extract the salt for reapplication. Finally, a week or so later, a loop of wire will be tied around its ankle and the ham will be ready to hang inside the house. Time, a little smoke and the cool mountain air will take care of the rest.

In two to three years, our Master's Well ham will mature into something much more desirable. That's too long for us, though, so Farmer Yang goes to fetch another leg that he salted two years earlier.

Eventually, ham number two arrives in the arms of another son. It's immediately clear that time has brought some changes to the ham. Its outer surface has darkened and dulled to the colour of baked mud – rusty, crusty and calcified – and it's dotted with little islands of pale mould. It's also about a third smaller than its original size, thanks to salt leeching out the moisture.

'We'll go to cook in their new house,' Zhang says, swatting a fly, 'away from the animals.' A pair of protesting chickens are picked up by the legs, a basket is filled with fresh eggs, and Farmer Yang's granddaughter exchanges the baby goat she's been cradling for an old cooking oil bottle filled with liquor, mixed with what at first glance appears to be hundreds of little yellow flowers. On closer inspection, they're wasps. Wasp, snake and lizard liquors are said to be good for men's health – in Yunnan, at least.

Our procession marches down the hill and across a covered wooden bridge, past cherry blossoms and curious dogs.

The Yangs' new house is a modern construction painted Bai white, with glass windows, a balcony, a neatly swept yard and an outside toilet. We gather in the yard under a deep blue sky, and soon a fire is crackling contentedly on the concrete outside the house. One of Farmer Yang's sons takes our ham and starts the process of waking it up from its two-year slumber.

HOW TO PREPARE A
YUNNAN HAM FOR EATING

STEP 1: SCORCHING Farmer Yang's son scorches the ham black over an open fire in the yard. In my childhood, I watched pig's heads and feet get scorched plenty of times. It is done to remove fine hair particles before chopping the meat into bite-sized chunks for cooking. Scorching kills off bacteria on the ham's surface, but nowadays this process is typically done so far away from supermarkets that most people never know about it. A little fat seeps out and caramelises on the wood, the rich scent wafting intermittently like snatches of music in the wind. It's the first blink of an awakened ham, coming out after its hibernation in a smoky barn in Master's Well Village.

STEP 2: CLEANING Blackened from trotter to buttock, the ham is removed from the flames and soaked in fresh, cold spring water, then scrubbed vigorously using a wire scouring brush and the sharp edge of a cleaver. About fifteen minutes of rigorous attention later, the ham emerges anew, sparkling like amber and ready for the final show. The blackened water drains into the vegetable patch outside the house.

STEP 3: CUTTING As one of the senior men present, Salt Maker Yang sets about carving the ham. Neighbours crane their necks over the wall to watch as he uses a cleaver to set a neat cutting line, and then uses a *kan chai dao*, a narrow blade somewhere between sword and axe, to hack cleanly through skin, flesh and bone, chopping the ham into straight-edged chunks of about 2 *jin* (1 kilogram).

STEP 4: STORING Once the ham is cut, the curing process stops completely. It is best to store the ham chunks in a refrigerator and consume within three months.

Crack, crunch, thunk. Yang's chopping is music in these parts, a sound that signals celebration and plenty. He turns a chunk of ham flesh-side up to display the cut surface. Everybody cranes their heads to look; a neat cross-section draws a collective sigh of appreciation from the spectators. It seems that this show of skill is as important in Bai village life as carving the Thanksgiving turkey is in the US.

We examine the jewelled interior: velvet-red meat patterned with seams of fat like the finest Dali marble. Time has done its work.

'See, every villager here knows how to make and prepare a ham!' exclaims Zhang triumphantly. 'This is a salt village – it's the culture.'

Our ham is butchered into chunks, with one sizeable slab set aside for lunch. The whole process from burning to chopping takes a good hour. 'It takes about 10 minutes to cure a ham, but it takes a lot longer to prepare it for eating.' Zhang comments, discounting the years in between.

A sliver of milky white fat is trimmed from the edge and tossed into an iron wok warming on the remains of the fire. Salt Maker Yang then roughly chops our slab into chunks and drops them into a pot of simmering water.

By now, the ham fat in the wok is opaque and bubbling. *Jue cai*, a stalky green fern from the mountains, is tossed in, and it also starts to sizzle and steam. A moment earlier, Salt Maker Yang was hacking through flesh and bone. Now his muscular arms delicately prepare the ferns, which transmute into a brilliant jade against the coal-black seasoned wok. It's a process to which he devotes all his attention, as if nothing matters at this moment besides the ritual of cooking.

A low, square table is placed a few metres from the fire, bordered by four simple bench seats. Out come the eggs, fried by Farmer Yang's daughter in lots of hot oil so that the whites have fluffed and crisped delightfully at the edges, while the yolks have remained tender to the touch. More vegetables in enamel dishware are served; bottles of Dali beer are uncapped and candles are lit to keep the flies away. Finally, the table receives its centrepiece: our ham, boiled and presented simply in a dented aluminium bowl.

For the second time today, all is quiet. I notice the faint gurgling of the stream as we chew and savour the food. High above, a herd of white goats moves slowly and silently along the steep mountainside. It could be Farmer Yang's wife leading them, Zhang says. But we're too far away to tell.

So what of our ham? It is Bai mountain food at its most primal and unadulterated. Some pieces are thick, others thin; some are dark and gamey, others pale and sweet.

We pick out the chunks we fancy with our chopsticks, each little more than a mouthful, and eat them over fluffy white rice. The boiling has mellowed the saltiness. The meat is chewy and rich, fatty and unadorned. It marries perfectly with the fresh eggs, making this meal a sort of pastoral Yunnanese version of bacon and eggs.

Bacon and eggs is a dish I rarely eat, and if I do I only ever manage one egg. Today, for reasons I can't quite explain, I eat three.

MASTER'S WELL BOILED HAM

炖火腿

SERVES 6–8

Eating glazed Virginia ham by the slice, or a juicy grilled steak or chicken breast, is quite different from the way Chinese ham is eaten.

For reasons of economy and health, meat in China is mostly chopped, diced or ground, and eaten more sparingly together with an array of other ingredients, such as in stir-fry, stew or soup. Peking duck and Cantonese roast meat are obvious exceptions, but they are often the main 'meaty' component on a table spread with copious vegetable dishes, fish, soup, tofu, greens and so on.

On China's less meat-centric dinner table (although this too is changing), Yunnan ham often plays a more minor but nevertheless vital gastronomic role. It's the ultimate meaty condiment when added sparingly to other dishes to impart a salty-sweet richness, or when relieved of its fat for frying and its bones for stock. The closer you are to ham-producing regions, however, the more simply one eats ham. It is often just soaked and stewed for hours to leach out the salt before being consumed in hefty, delicious mouthfuls. It seems almost primal or wasteful to eat ham in such chunks, but they are extremely satisfying, particularly in the fresh mountain setting.

1.1kg ham, skin on

2 cups water

Slice ham into 2cm-by-5cm slices, 1cm thick.

Toss ham into a pot, add cold water, bring to a boil, and stew for 30 minutes over medium heat. (Water quantity is dependent on the saltiness of the ham; the saltier it is, the more water is needed.)

Scoop ham slices into a bowl. Serve hot or at room temperature.

MASTER'S WELL FRIED FERN WITH HAM

火腿炒蕨菜

SERVES 6–8

Edible ferns grow widely in China and Japan. Tender curly stems fresh out of the soil, commonly known as fiddleheads in western cuisine, are considered delicacies. Herders and farmers often pick these stems on their way home to supplement dinner. In spring, villagers often go to the mountains to pick a larger quantity to dry for future use. Here we are cooking with freshly picked stems.

Picking ferns is a skill developed with experience. You pinch the stem with the nails of your index finger and thumb, 10 to 12 centimetres from the tip; if the stem snaps off easily, that's a good sign. It means the stem is tender and edible. If your nails cannot break it, then move another couple of centimetres toward the tip and try again. Freshly picked fern should be boiled and soaked overnight in cold water to release the bitter taste, along with any toxins that come from the soil.

1.3kg boiled and soaked fern stems, cut into 3cm segments

200g fatty ham

3 dried chili peppers, whole or cut into 3cm segments for stronger flavour (optional)

Toss ham into a wok heated over medium heat; stir until smoky and the fat has been released.

Add chilli to wok, cook until chilli turns golden brown.

Add fern pieces to wok, turn the heat up high, and stir. Cook until the liquid from the ferns evaporates (about 2–3 minutes).

Scoop into a bowl and serve hot or at room temperature.

A HERD OF GOATS

'NOW THAT you have your ham, we can head back to town for dinner,' Zhang says. How he can think about dinner right after such an elaborate lunch is beyond my comprehension, but this is standard Yunnan hospitality; Zhang just takes it a little further.

Zhang and I first met on a trip I made to Yunnan a few months ago. When I called to ask for his help on my quest for a ham, I did not know that he would go to such lengths, taking three full days out of his schedule, accompanying us in his own jeep, and arranging every one of our meals. 'This is how Yunlong people always treat a visitor, stranger or not.' Zhang told us proudly.

The first words out of Zhang's mouth are usually, 'Have you eaten?' They are closely followed by the obligatory offering of a cigarette. He has a lively, inquiring face, leant an academic air by a pair of spectacles.

Zhang is the owner of a *nong jia le* (农家乐), literally 'Farm House Happiness', a type of traveller's experience – usually in the form of a simple restaurant and sometimes with an attached guesthouse – that rural China has adopted with some success, offering city folk a taste of the old ways, including home-cooked farm food, mountain vistas and plenty of open space.

The name of Zhang's *nong jia le* is Yi Wo Yang (一窝羊), A Herd of Goats, and it is nestled at the foot of the hill atop which sits the village of Nuodeng, just a little way north of Yunlong town. After a day of adventure in the salt and ham villages, it's comforting to return to Zhang's home base and know that things are taken care of.

It's late afternoon when we wander past his nearly built guesthouse, painted bright orange like a Spanish hacienda and supported by stout, red, wooden pillars. A dry wall of bricks is inset attractively with old millstones, weathered timber and faded carvings from another age.

Zhang is like a magpie for curios, a scavenger of remote villages, always eager to offer a farmer a few *yuan* for an interestingly carved roof tile that's just lying around. The old loom from Farmer Yang's house and a sculpted brick from Salt Maker Yang's house have made their way back to A Herd of Goats with us, now part of the collection.

A condemned goat has also come back with us, strapped, bleating, inside the back of Zhang's jeep. A local party has made reservations for a whole roasted goat,

Zhang tells us. I feel sorry for the beast, but happy for Zhang's booming business. On his vegetable patch beside the river, Zhang grows cucumbers, pumpkins, chillies, radishes, cabbages, bitter melons and more.

A Herd of Goats is a popular *nong jia le*. The dishes are reasonably priced and really tasty, but I suspect its popularity is really due to Zhang's gift of the gab. He knows everybody – what they like to eat, on what days and with whom. Driving around Yunlong on our journey, Zhang would often pull over to greet a driver in a passing car. He'd invite them to visit – *'Guo lai zuo!'* – and conclude with a nod of the head in the direction we were heading and a *'Zou le ga.'* Literally, 'I'd better be off.'

Zhang is the sort of driven entrepreneur one often encounters in rural counties. He has no office hours, but he's at his restaurant by 7:30 every morning. He smokes and drinks green tea, but doesn't eat much. He worries about our breakfast, our lunch on the road, and insists on feeding us every evening. Dinner often stretches late into the night, extended by chatting, smoking and drinking Zhang's home-infused corn liquor.

'I never drink during the day,' Zhang tells me. 'It messes things up.' Case in point is his quiet sidekick, Mr Yang (another Yang!), who runs the kitchen at A Herd of Goats. 'See him?' Zhang says. 'He's been with me for ten years. He was a drunk before, so his wife left him and he was depressed. I gave him a job, but asked for one commitment from him: no drinking during the day. He stayed true to his word. Still, he enjoys his drink at night, but that's fine.'

The ever-resourceful Zhang doesn't stop at being a restaurateur; he has taken his enterprise to the next level. He shows us into his alcohol room, where dozens of enormous clay jars of corn and millet alcohol sit in rows, averaging a potent 92 to 96 proof. We enter another barnyard to see even more booze in jars beneath tiered shelves. Zhang prints his own labels, which tread a smart line between rustic and stylish; he has a strong sense of branding. In an enormous tub filled with alcohol, large pieces of wood float like the aftermath of a shipwreck. 'I'm pickling the wood to make furniture,' explains Zhang. 'It protects the wood from disease and rot.'

Zhang has saved the best for last, however: his ham house. Inside a small, lattice-framed structure, over one hundred hams hang in the well-ventilated darkness. A dry, savoury aroma fills the room. Zhang buys pork from nearby villages and cures it himself, helped by his staff of ten.

When we discuss the price of ham, Zhang shakes his head. Ever since Nuodeng was featured on *A Bite of China*, demand for local ham has skyrocketed. Nuodeng ham was the star of the first episode, where it was diced and fried with white rice, as well as sautéed with *wosun*, a thick-stemmed lettuce also known as celtuce or Chinese lettuce. Most Chinese people had already heard of Xuanwei ham, but the high quality of Nuodeng ham was news to many. Immediately, Nuodeng hams tripled in price.

Regardless, we have to see Nuodeng for ourselves. As Zhang busies himself with dinner, we head off for a late afternoon visit.

NUODENG

THE ENTIRE road leading from A Herd of Goats up to Nuodeng looks like a construction site. It's a struggle to navigate even the 3-kilometre distance, but when we finally get there, we find a beautiful village.

Grand houses of terracotta sandstone bricks soar up the mountainside in cake-like layers. The pitch is so extreme that it's as if the houses are built directly on top of one another. In fact, many are connected. As we climb the steep stone steps that run through the village, we spot hand-painted wooden signs directing visitors to guesthouses and restaurants. We pass a small shop selling ice cream, soft drinks and vacuum-sealed chunks of Nuodeng ham.

By now we have slogged our way up the steep valley, and we are in desperate need of refreshment. The veranda of Bieyuan Guesthouse beckons, a charming old home with gorgeous mountain views. Collapsing on to garden furniture, we order something to drink, and the owner comes out to chat. A young Chinese man from Wuhan, he has a fleshy, babyish face, a gentle voice and a delicate manner. He's dressed in what appears to be colourful new age pyjamas and sandals.

We ask him about business and tourism in general. He explains that a new road is currently being constructed into the village – a prospect he isn't all that keen on. 'Now, Nuodeng is a special place. The types of people finding their way here are independent travellers looking for culture and history. But if Nuodeng starts attracting mass tourism, I won't even be able to walk down the mountain anymore!'

Sitting in the cobbled courtyard on the side of a mountain, we drink in the vista of green-forested mountains and elegant, grey-tiled rooftops – a picture of rusticated prosperity with not a single modern building blighting the view.

Paradoxically, a flood of tourists wouldn't necessarily do much for Nuodeng's guesthouse business. Most tourists would be day-trippers, touching down in Nuodeng as part of a bus tour, then heading somewhere else for cookie-cutter accommodations and evening entertainment. Tranquillity and idleness are usually a tough sell for big, busy bus groups.

With the day almost gone, we descend gingerly through the steep alleyways back to Zhang's house for dinner. We leave behind a dreamlike rural village on the verge of joining the outside world, with all the changes and unknowns that go along with that.

Zhang's kitchen has a corrugated roof and a stone floor. It's fastidiously clean and organised. There is a cooler filled with vegetables and meat; an old medicine cabinet contains spices, chillies, pickles and dried goods. A piece of our ham has been stewing for hours on a tiled stove that is loaded with wood from just outside.

Zhang's chef removes the ham chunks with a large ladle and cleaves through the soft meat on a round butcher's block. The fat glistens like the bronzed skin of a Peking duck. When people eat ham in Yunnan, it needs to have plenty of fat attached to the lean meat, which makes the meat tastier.

With our photographer, Liz, shooting the action in the kitchen, Zhang, ever watchful and aware of our needs, quips to his chef, 'Hey, move those pieces around so the view is better. You're becoming famous now. Don't lose your nerve!'

Pretty soon Zhang is directing the whole enterprise – both the cooking and the photography. His enthusiasm is infectious; his staff just about manages to keep their cool as their boss enlists them to be production assistants in the photo shoot that has taken over the kitchen.

Slices of stewed meat gently simmer for a few more minutes. The chef lightly whips some fresh eggs, barely breaking the yolk, then pours them over the simmering meat.

Out in the yard, a table is set under the shade of a banyan tree, whose leaves form a jade canopy overhead. Locals call the banyan *huang jiao shu* – Yellow Horn Tree – for its edible golden leaf buds that have a startlingly sour taste. It's evening now. The temperature is dropping and the air is becoming sweeter.

Our dish arrives, a hash of soft, fatty ham, eggs with vivid golden yolks and a rich sauce made from the thickened cooking broth. It's accompanied by rice, a simple mint salad and stir-fried vegetables from the garden.

'I learned this dish from a local family in a village,' Zhang explains. 'I just go places and watch. I pay attention to what people cook, the condiments they use, even the brands of oil. It's people who are the carriers of culture.' To me, this dish represents Zhang – his restless curiosity and amateur anthropology.

As we sip Zhang's corn liquor, he tells me more about himself. Now nearing 50, he's prone to a bit of introspection. He started out on his own in 1993, 'jumping into the sea', as he calls it, selling local produce like dried wood-ear mushrooms and tree lichen. People elsewhere in China were becoming interested in the exotic mountain treasures of Yunnan at that time. He even partnered with a scientist to find a method of preserving rhododendron petals as an edible delicacy to expand his product portfolio.

But in recent years, fewer and fewer people have been willing to forage for lichens and rare produce, preferring instead to live and work in cities. That's why Zhang decided to open A Herd of Goats. Now, people from all walks of life have been turning up at his place with new ideas. Which, for a curious mind like Zhang's, is perfect.

I ask him how he chose the name 'A Herd of Goats'.

'A herd of goats means abundance. If it's just one goat, you eat it and it's gone, but a herd will always produce more goats.'

EGG HAM HASH

火腿炖土鸡蛋

SERVES 4–6

This is an unusual dish that I have only had at A Herd of Goats. In other parts of Yunnan, a different form of this dish highlights the egg soup more, and uses finely diced ham just to add flavour. When it's egg-focused, this dish is called Yunnan Ham and Osmanthus Egg, because the floating pieces of egg are supposed to look like little white Osmanthus flowers, a lovely fragrant flower in southern China.

However, this recipe follows Zhang's preference and uses a larger portion of ham.

200g ham, skin on

4 cups water

4 eggs

Submerge the whole chunk of ham in cold water, bring to a boil, and stew for 2 hours over low heat. (The quantity of water depends on the saltiness of the ham; the saltier it is, the more water is needed.)

Slice ham into 3cm-by-5cm slices, 1cm thick; put in a cooking pot.

Add 1½ cups of ham stock from the earlier ham boiling, bringing to a boil again.

Break 4 eggs in a separate bowl, mix lightly, and slowly pour the egg mixture in a constant stream into the boiling stock. The eggs will form little white clusters on top of the ham and stock. Turn the heat to high and bring to a boil again for 2–3 minutes; serve hot or at room temperature.

STEAMED HAM SLICE

蒸火腿

SERVES 4–6

This dish is very similar to the one from Master's Well Village, but this one produces a nice ham stock. The long, two-hour cooking time also releases more fat and salt from the ham, making this dish less oily than a straight boiled ham dish. We also eat the skin which, after a long simmer, practically melts in your mouth.

300g ham, skin on

4 cups water

Submerge the whole chunk of ham in cold water, bring to a boil over high heat, then stew for 2 hours over low heat. (The quantity of water depends on the saltiness of the ham; the saltier it is, the more water is needed.)

Slice ham into 3cm-by-5cm slices, 1cm thick; arrange on a plate.

Steam for 10 minutes before serving.

HAM KNUCKLE DAIKON STEW

火腿蹄炖萝卜

SERVES 4–6

This is, again, a very simple use of the ham. A lot of locals prefer this ham knuckle stew over straight boiled ham because the thick skin on the ham knuckle gives it a chewy texture, which is the perfect accompaniment to drinking strong local liquor.

500g ham knuckle, bone in, skin on, chopped into 3cm pieces

Scrub and clean the ham knuckle thoroughly, and chop into pieces.

4 cups water

1kg daikon (or any root vegetable, like yam, potato, etc.), cut into 3cm chunks

Submerge ham knuckle in water, bring to a boil, and stew over low heat for 2 hours. (The quantity of water depends on the saltiness of the ham; the saltier it is, the more water is needed.)

Add daikon to stew, increase heat and bring to a boil again. Simmer over low heat for another 30 minutes. Remove from heat; serve hot or at room temperature.

MINT SALAD

凉拌薄荷

SERVES 4–6

Unique to Chinese cuisine and medicine, the 'energy properties' of food are considered alongside nutrition and taste. Food is mostly identified as 'heating' (*yang*) or 'cooling' (*yin*), which refers to the food's capacity to generate either hot or cold energy in the body. This energy is different from temperature or spice; it's only the effect it has on the body. If your body has hot energy, then eating 'heating' food may cause an uncomfortable eruption of mouth ulcers, dry tongue, etc. If your body has cold energy, then eating 'cooling' food may cause nausea and even fainting. It's important to find a *yin-yang* balance in food and body.

By this theory, ham is a heating food, so it's no surprise that Zhang chooses a mint salad, which is cooling, to accompany the ham dish.

---

2 cups tender mint tips, loosely packed

½ tbsp white vinegar

2 tbsp cold water

½ tsp salt, or to taste

1 tsp soy sauce

2 cloves garlic, finely chopped

1 dried chilli pepper, roasted over an open fire, finely crushed

Rinse mint in cold water, place all ingredients in a bowl; toss and serve cold.

A TALE OF TWO VILLAGES

ZHANG INSISTS on feeding us breakfast at his restaurant before we head to Shundang, another salt village. After a bowl of noodles, we get back into the car, this time passing the turnoff for Master's Well Village and continuing further north along Bi River.

We drive until we spot a scattering of red and purple paper on the roadside. We also see a pair of white scrolls posted on both sides of a gate. Crowds gather inside the gate. Obviously, a funeral is underway. We pull over to investigate further.

Zhang makes a few inquiries and discovers that the deceased in this case was the elderly father of the local middle school principal. This morning his body was conveyed down the mountain from his hillside home for cremation. A scattering of spent firecrackers and paper flowers runs across an old, covered wooden bridge and up a steep riverside path, like a trail of breadcrumbs.

When an old person dies in China, a funeral is both a celebration as well as an occasion for mourning. When my grandmother passed away years ago, I learned that there are two important celebrations in Chinese life: the red celebration and the white celebration. The red one is a wedding, and the white one is a funeral for someone who has lived past 80. What unites the two is the gathering of family and friends around good food and wine. The main difference is really just colour; a Chinese bride wears red, and everything is decorated red, as red will fend off any evil spirits. At a white funeral, the mourning colour is white, as pure as he or she was upon entering the world.

We walk along the trail, leaving the modern roadside buildings behind. The path takes us over another covered bridge toward the old village Shundang where the deceased lived and died. It's a hot march in the morning sun. The path winds up to a ridge, upon which is perched a remarkable stone watchtower, old but solid, with tapering eaves. On the side of an old stone arch, a decades-old poster prevails on villagers to 'Fight the Drought'. Another patch of text, dated 1951, proclaims that the people have risen up to become the masters. The writing is so faded that it takes quite a bit effort to make out.

A teacher from the school, another Mr Yang, accompanies us. Teacher Yang explains that Shundang, like Master's Well Village, is one of the eight famed salt wells of Yunlong. That salt was once such a valuable commodity in these parts is made evident by the imposing, Qing-era fortifications that protect the path leading into the village. Teacher Yang explains that soldiers were once posted here to guard against salt thieves.

We approach a beautiful timber house that belonged to a wealthy salt merchant. Later, the owner was relocated and the house was converted by the government for grain storage. The family that owns it now leaves it locked up and semi-derelict; they live in a new concrete home down by the road. In fact, on closer inspection, most of the houses here have rotting timber foundations. Mud and stones have tumbled into the homes, and – save for a few places occupied by residents too old or poor to move – everyone seems to have departed.

Clucking hens are about the only sign of life we see until two boys peek their heads over the wall of a simple Bon temple in the centre of the village. The Bai in villages like these worship local gods. A pair of gaudily painted temple guardians flank the entrance.

Shundang came into being during the Ming Dynasty, Teacher Yang explains. The village's original salt well is still intact. It's still in use, actually, though all is quiet today because of the funeral.

We are about to make our way back down to the river when we hear a voice and see an old man shuffling out of his century-old, two-storey timber and mud house. He's wearing a cap and an old police jacket in a washed out shade of blue. A few white whiskers poke out from his dark face. Old Zhao is 65 years old. He is a salt maker.

Enthusiastically, Old Zhao tells us the village legend – how a shepherd boy from beyond the valley lost his sheep and tracked them all the way to what would become the village of Shundang. The sheep had drunk deeply from a spring – so deeply, in fact, that the salty water had killed them. And so it was discovered that the hillside was rich in salt.

As the crow flies, Master's Well Village is only 55 kilometres from here, over green mountains and river valleys. Nevertheless, the Bai dialect spoken in Shundang is entirely different from that spoken in Master's Well Village. Even Zhang needs Teacher Yang to interpret Old Zhao's story.

Old Zhao is one of the last remaining residents of this village. Like many remote Bai villages in Dali Prefecture, Shundang is a tale of two settlements. The original village, of pretty and sometimes even magnificent stone farmhouses that were built with old salt wealth, is quietly tucked up the mountain on the side of the river further

from the road. Over time, inhabitants have migrated across the river to build a newer village with concrete block houses beside the road. Many have invested in cars and motorbikes. A connection to the outside world trumps picturesque scenery.

Old Zhao walks with us a little way, and the precise story of the village's decline begins to unfold. In the summer of 1978, a sinkhole was discovered higher up in the mountain. A young geologist arrived from Kunming and explained that centuries of well digging had rendered the ground dangerously unstable. Villagers grew worried and the exodus began, compounded by the decline of the salt trade, the lure of modern housing and proximity to the local school.

I marvel at how different Shundang is from Master's Well Village. Master's Well was teeming with life; newborns in the barns and the houses; shepherds on the hillsides; workers sweating over salt brine pans; kids playing basketball and spinning tops. People there have pride and conviction in their traditions. Not to mention ubiquitous mobile phone coverages. Shundang, in contrast, is a quiet echo of its former glory.

But as we leave the village, passing funeral flowers of yellow and white paper pinned to the bushes, we spy hints of a future for Shundang. We see a preservation plaque on the old watchtower, and blue, solar-powered street lamps. It might be a fiver-hour drive from the nearest airport, but Shundang has potential as a living museum of a bygone era. Perhaps one day soon this fading village might have something more than funerals to celebrate.

JIANCHUAN COUNTY

SHAXI, CHEESE AND
MOUNTAIN TUNES

LEAVING BEHIND the salt wells, covered bridges and all those Yangs of Yunlong, we continue north and then east into Jianchuan County. Now we are out of ham country and into the land of woodcarvers.

Since my childhood, the word 'Jianchuan' has often been a prefix to something else, as in *'jianchuan mujiang'* (Jianchuan wood worker), *'jianchuan shibaoshan'* (Jianchuan Shibaoshan Grottoes), or *'jianchuan shibaoshan gehui'* (Jianchuan Shibaoshan Folk Song Festival).

For me, these phrases used to neatly sum up Jianchuan's identity. The skill of Jianchuan wood workers is coveted all the way south to the tropical regions of Xishuangbanna and all the way north to Tibet. And the grottoes and folk singing are also important elements of Jianchuan culture.

However, with time I began to see another side of Jianchuan and its residents. The Bai, in addition to being studious and hardworking, have a surprisingly free spirit that worships and talks openly about love and sex.

Within the Shibaoshan Grottoes, Jianchuan's earlier craftsman carved, in sandstone, the popular sculpture Ah-Yang-Bai, a giant vagina flanked by various protective gods. Hoping to become pregnant, married couples come from far away to give Ah-Yang-Bai a gentle rub for luck. The sculpture glistens like a polished door-knob, smoothed by centuries of hopeful hands. I gave Ah-Yang-Bai a rub in 2001. My son was born a year later.

Every year from July to September, Jianchuan becomes the Woodstock of Dali. Tens of thousands of Bai people gather on Shibaoshan Mountain for a folk song festival that lasts two months. Besides visiting Ah-Yang-Bai, the crowds scatter all over the mountain, cooking outside, dancing in meadows and camping out at night. The main attraction of the festival is a folk song singing competition, but it is rumoured that the forests and rocks also provide the perfect cover for all sorts of hanky-panky at night.

I wonder if that has something to do with the power of Ah-Yang-Bai.

For any noteworthy folk singer, the ultimate stage is the one located on Sideng Street in Shaxi, at the foot of Shibaoshan Mountain. We have made plans to visit that stage on this trip.

But first we speed up the winding road, past the Shibaoshan Grottoes, on our way to meet a local folk song king.

MOUNTAIN TUNES IN
STONE DRAGON VILLAGE

THERE'S A saying about the children of Stone Dragon Village: Those who can walk, dance; and those who can talk, sing. About 100 kilometres from Shundang, in a high mountain valley beside an oval lake, Stone Dragon Village is home to roughly 1000 Bai people. I had been told there was a Bai folksong expert in the village, so I arranged to stop by on our way to Shaxi.

Chief Li, the head of Stone Dragon Village, receives us in a concrete yard belonging to the local government office. Tea is served: the usual scattering of leaves in a paper cup and hot water from a thermos. A bland atmosphere of bureaucracy pervades the place, which seems to extend to Li himself, a short, slight man in his fifties wearing the semi-formal attire of a government official – a grey suit with no tie. Stone Dragon Village, he explains seriously in a soft, muffled voice, is a place of song. The musical tradition runs deep.

His claims, including the one that he himself is known as the 'Folk Music King', seem a little silly in this official setting.

And then a transformation takes place.

Three dancing girls emerge from a small office, two of them in traditional dress wielding *ba wang bian* (霸王鞭), bamboo staffs as long as golf clubs and inset with bells. A young male singer comes outside, dark-skinned and heavy-set, oily black hair parted to the right, carrying a three-stringed guitar slung low on his hip. His name is also Li, so for ease of identification I shall call him 'Elvis'. Elvis picks out a driving rhythm as the girls twirl seductively and clack the *ba wang bian* against their feet, shoulders, hips and the ground. This is a dance that I have seen many times before, but I had no idea that it originated from Stone Dragon Village.

Elvis starts to sing in a glassy tenor with a rough edge, maintaining a rhythm a shade slower than that of a resting heartbeat, occasionally tossing his head to clear the tousled hair from his eyes. Utterly in the moment, he possesses swagger and sex appeal that is quite unexpected given the surroundings. In another context he could be a stage performer of real gravitas – a rock star. A few tourists drift in from the street to watch. A dog scratches about in the dirt nearby.

Soon Elvis is joined by a woman, her shrill soprano cutting through the late afternoon air. As they sing together in the local Bai dialect, Li leans in and whispers the words in Mandarin for my benefit. The lyrics are sensual and provocative, about longing and lust, wantonness and excitement. It's captivating. Elvis's three unamplified strings keep rhythm and add a mournful melody in between verses.

There are many types of Bai tunes, Chief Li explains: nursery rhymes, love songs, working songs, songs to commemorate historical legends, songs for funerals and songs for weddings. Practically any occasion can call for a song.

'Of all the different forms of Bai folks songs,' says Li, 'it's love songs that are sung the most.' With a grin, he points out that even today, men sometimes attempt to woo women with song. 'They follow the women on their way to the fields, walking behind them and singing as they go.'

As the village head, Chief Li also uses song as a vehicle for delivering official news and government information sent all the way from Beijing. 'It helps the villagers take notice if we sing the information to them,' he explains.

In a sparse office beside us, a man memorises Chinese characters hand-written on a sheet of purple funerary paper. It has been folded, fan-like, to create rows of narrow columns that contain the characters in vertical lines. Li wrote the lyrics, and this man is learning them so he can sing at a funeral later this evening. The poem has been written specially for the occasion, laying out the virtues of the deceased man. After the recital, the paper will be burned. The same ritual probably also took place for the funeral back in Shundang.

Now, would we like to hear Chief Li sing?

He steps away for a moment, then re-emerges from his office, his jacket replaced with a colourful, folksy waistcoat. But his transformation goes far beyond apparel. As Li takes the guitar and sings a song about love, his vocal chords let loose, revealing a rich, gravelly voice imbued with sadness, wisdom and romance. The façade of government formality disappears.

He sings another song, 'The Mud Fish'. The lyrics are from the perspective of a fish that is about to be eaten, but in reality it's a lament about the lot of the humble farmer. The pain is audible in Li's voice and visible in his eyes. He might be just a little fish, Chief Li sings, but at least his bones will scratch the throats of his masters on the way down.

THE MUD FISH SONG

Fine-scaled little fish is scared,
Sometimes there is the rice paddy but no water.
Sometimes there is water but no rice paddy to live in,
I can only hide beneath the water-weed.

But I can't hide every day,
I just venture out and I get caught.
Someone stuffs me inside the fishing basket,
Wiggle, wiggle, I suffer.

The man says deep-fry,
The woman says marinate.
Served on a plate,
They invite each other to pick at me.

The one who catches me will go blind,
The one who eats me will fall down.
Although I am powerless to fight,
My bones will choke him.

泥鳅调

细鳞鱼儿惊惶惶
有了地盘没水养
有了水养没地盘
水草下面藏

天天躲藏憋不住
刚刚出门被捉翻
将我塞进鱼篓里
挣扎受熬煎

汉子说是要做煎
婆娘说是要做腌
将我摆在席面上
邀来邀去拣

捉我那个眼要瞎
吃我那个要倒塌
纵虽无力来反抗
要用刺卡他

Li's voice is mesmerising. To look at this quiet man in his shirt and waistcoat, you'd never guess he is a repository of musical knowledge, of love songs, of flirtatious and salacious ballads, of odes, tragedies and comedic word play.

Li was identified in 1999 as a folk singing talent cultivated by the provincial government, he tells me after the performance. He himself has subsequently found and nurtured a female singer – the 'Folk Song Queen' to his King – and they perform together with a troupe at weddings and, in the case of this evening, funerals.

Did Chief Li woo his own wife through songs?

'No,' he admits, 'I was betrothed before birth. My marriage to my wife was arranged while both our mothers were pregnant, as used to be custom in Stone Dragon Village.' Li goes on, 'In the countryside you have to respect these customs. When I was growing up, even if I liked other girls, I could never date them because I knew I had a wife waiting for me.'

Now he spends most of his time performing, whether for local events or for the small but growing number of tourists finding their way to Stone Dragon Village.

Folk traditions are not as strong as they once were, Li tells me. When he was a boy he didn't have TV or even electricity to keep him occupied, unlike kids today. Without TV, video games, and the Internet, music was his entertainment.

In fact, a big part of Li's work is promoting the folk singing culture of his people. But it's not easy persuading children to learn the songs and musicianship of yesteryear. The provincial government gave him funds to convert an old office into classrooms for local kids to learn singing and dancing. At first it didn't work. 'No one came,' Li says mournfully. But all was not lost. Once he offered children a small stipend to show up, they started attending. Soon he had over 120 pupils and was turning more away.

Elvis steps up to sing a few more songs as the daylight fades. He is all smiles and swagger. After he finishes, I ask him what the Chinese name is for his folk guitar. He tells me it's called a *san xian* (三弦), or three strings, and then explains solemnly that I shouldn't think of it as a musical instrument. 'What is it, then?' I dutifully ask.

'A love rifle,' he says with a wink.

THE SALT SONG

We listened to many songs that afternoon, all in the Bai dialect. One of them happened to be an old folk song about salt makers, which I had to include here. The song describes the lifestyle of salt carriers in Yunlong County. It also describes the trading route to more developed areas of Dali like those around Shaxi.

I couldn't find a written source for the song, and unfortunately Bai is an oral language that I can't speak, but luckily when I called Li a few months later, he had neatly recorded it on a piece of paper, just like the funeral song. He had one of his assistants photograph it and text it to me in Beijing:

SALT PORTER'S SONG

The east is just turning white; the day is about to break,
Little sister, are you going to carry salt?
If my little sister is going to carry salt,
I'll wait for you at Yunlong.
We can go together to carry salt.
We carry salt to Heqing to trade for oil and rice.
Because we are poor.
We have to do it no matter how hard it is.
My good little sister, my good little sister,
Pause for a break at Bali Bridge.
Let's have lunch in Mapingguan Village,
I, your big brother, will bring lunch for both of us.
We can carry on after lunch,
We'll sleep for the night in Sideng Street.
There is no work to do in the evening,
So we can watch opera at the ancient stage.

背盐调

东方发白天就亮
妹子是否去背盐
妹子若是去背盐
在云龙等你
咱俩一同去背盐
背到鹤庆换油米
只因咱家里贫穷
辛苦也得去
好妹子呀好妹子
到八里桥闲一闲
马平关吃中午饭
午饭哥带起
午饭后继续赶路
到寺登街投宿去
夜晚咱没事情干
古戏台看戏

Note: Sideng Street is in Shaxi, and the opera stage is still standing. In Yunnan, 'little sister' is an endearing term for a young girl. A young man who is slightly older would be called 'ge', or big brother. And with regards to the line about resting on the bridge, Yunlong's many covered bridges are designed with seats along both sides to allow merchants and porters to rest along their journeys.

THE CHEESE MAKER

WE LEAVE Stone Dragon Village and head twenty minutes down the road to the main attraction – Shaxi. We bed down for the night in an inn. The next day, in the morning sunlight, we bring our leg of ham through groomed fields, past the old wooden gates of Shaxi, to the farmhouse of Mrs Shi Fumei.

Shi's farmhouse is spotless. A traditional Bai building, its enclosing courtyard walls are freshly whitewashed, the floor is swept, and everything is in its place. The sheer number of cultivated plants and flowers in the yard, perfectly trimmed and tended, is astonishing. Orchids and peonies gaze skyward from under a taut black fly shade. Decorative pine, winter jasmine, peaches, loquats, cherries, pomegranates, cinnamon and many other Chinese herbs I can't name, sit in neatly arranged pots.

A pair of pearlescent river fish hang drying from a beam. Rows of hams and *larou* (a Chinese version of bacon, cured in strips) are suspended from the wooden eaves, their bottoms wrapped in plastic bags to prevent oil from dripping on the ground. Even the teapot has a tiny cover made from a used medicine bottle on its spout to keep it clean.

Shi wears the uniform of rural domesticity: pants and a blouse under a neat blue apron, with patterned protectors over her sleeves. Her hair is tied back, but a few strands fall across her forehead. She has a shy, endearing smile and a quiet, dignified manner.

After introductions, Shi busies herself preparing tea. In the inner courtyard, an old man sits in his rocking chair, white hair combed back from his face. He is Shi's 88-year-old father-in-law. A beam of morning sun falls across his shoulders, catching the steam that spirals upwards from his tea. He reaches down to toss a cornhusk into the stove on the floor that's warming his feet. There are several more husks stacked neatly in a bowl beside him.

Shi's husband returns from the cowshed with a tin pail full of fresh milk. He wears simple cloth shoes, and sleeve protectors over his jacket. The milk is taken to the kitchen. We are going to make Chinese cheese.

In most parts of the country, Chinese people have little appetite for cheese. As a group, we are far more likely to be lactose intolerant than people of European descent. Instead of dairy, therefore, our powers of transmutation are largely employed to turn the humble soybean into countless iterations of tofu. A fermented variety known as *chou doufu* (臭豆腐) would probably be considered as alien and unappetising to most Western palates as blue cheese is to most Chinese ones.

That is not to say there isn't a culture of dairy consumption in China. Two of the last three ruling imperial dynasties – the Yuan (Mongol) and the Qing (Manchu) – were pastoral peoples from the great, grassy plains of northern China and Mongolia. Herding families subsist exclusively on the meat and milk of their sheep (or goats and yaks for Tibetans). In Beijing, little clay pots of yoghurt and milk are still delivered daily to shops on every street corner.

But Dali, thousands of kilometres from China's northern plains, boasts its own unique cheese culture, a remnant of earlier Mongolian influence. The Bai produce a fresh, ricotta-like cheese from goat's or cow's milk. It is usually fried and seasoned before eating, and often served together with strips of ham, the clean bite of the cheese balancing the oily richness of the meat. It's a delicious tapas plate of sorts that has come to exemplify Yunnan food in cities around China.

Like most Bai households in the Shaxi valley, Shi Fumei makes her own cheese from milk provided by her cows. Today she has agreed to show us how it's done.

SHI FUMEI'S CHEESE MAKING
PROCESS

STEP 1 The fresh milk is first steamed atop the wood-fired stove in Shi Fumei's immaculate country kitchen. In the mountains, goat's milk is most commonly used, which results in a stronger, gamier flavour, but Shi prefers the milder taste of cow's milk cheese. (I ask if she ever simply drinks the milk. 'Occasionally,' she says, 'but we filter it first.')

STEP 2 After about twenty minutes, it's time to separate the curds from the whey. Unlike ricotta, which typically uses vinegar to catalyse this process, Shi has created her own acid from a previous batch of whey (the liquid by-product of cheese making), which has been aging for two to three months in plastic bottles in the sun. Pouring two ladlefuls into the milk, we watch the curds cluster magically into little white islands.

STEP 3 The curds are then scooped into small square moulds lined with cloth, which she ties tightly together to squeeze out excess liquid. Shi repeats the process of tying and then untying four or five times, the hunks of pearly white cheese curds shrinking a little each time. Finally satisfied with the compressed blocks of cheese, Shi sets them down. 'They need about thirty minutes to cool completely. Otherwise, if you cut it now, it'll crumble.'

In between her farming and housekeeping duties, the remarkable Shi Fumei makes shoes. Her specialty is cloth shoes with sturdy rubber soles made from old tires, in a few simple styles and colours, either closed across the foot or open to the tops of the toes. Her husband helps out too, hand-carving the grip grooves in the rubber soles with a knife.

As we talk, Shi stitches a pair of shoes together on an old sewing machine, turning the spindle by rocking her feet rhythmically back and forth. The sewing machine was part of her dowry twenty years ago, she explains. It's been put to good use, too, as Shi's shoes have become the family's main source of income.

Her world – this perfect farmhouse that opens out on to a view of jade-green fields and rice terraces – seems idyllic to me, something to idolise and yearn for. The reality, Shi tells me, is that she's run off her feet every day and rarely finds time to do anything just for herself. On top of her farming duties and shoe making, there are the elderly parents to look after and the younger generation to raise – family responsibilities that are as demanding as they are rewarding. 'Sometimes,' she confesses, 'I feel trapped.'

Her grandson (more accurately, her brother-in-law's grandson) chases butterflies in the sun-dappled yard, toddling unsteadily on his little legs and laughing each time one comes close. Does Shi expect her children to stay in the village when they are older? 'It's okay if he doesn't return,' she says, referring to her eldest son who is currently away at university in Xi'an. Her second son attends the middle school in Shaxi. She gets up, announcing, 'The cheese will be ready now.'

Back in the kitchen, Shi opens one of the cheesecloth parcels to reveal a perfect, off-white cube. It's smooth-sided and lustrous, and she slices it uniformly with a large cleaver. The raw taste is mild, with a pleasant, ever-so-crumbly bite.

Shi goes upstairs and retrieves some pucks of hard brown sugar. The Chinese character *fu* (福) – meaning prosperity and good fortune – is carved on the tops of the sugar pucks. 'I will make you the dish I make for my son when he comes home to visit. It's his favourite. The thing he is always homesick for.'

I have specifically searched out a cheese maker who would be able to make a dish with my ham. I was expecting a straightforward dish of steamed ham and cheese, which is common in this part of the country, but Shi has other ideas. In addition to sugar, she's brought out other surprising ingredients: eggs and fermented sweet rice.

A large piece of our Master's Well ham is sliced up, together with shavings of the auspicious brown sugar. Shi pours a few centimetres of oil into a giant wok, the same one she used to steam the milk. The cheese slices are fried for a few seconds on each side until golden, then removed. The excess oil is then drained and stored for cooking other dishes. The ham goes in next, followed by a cup of fermented sweet rice, everything coming together in a stew-like mulch. Taken off the heat, the golden brown mixture is then steamed to further enrich the flavour.

Eaten over plain white rice, it's pure comfort food, like the hug of a cosy blanket. The saltiness of our ham cuts through the occasional crystal of sweet sugar, and the cheese adds substance. I can understand how the dish's candy sweetness lends it a nostalgic quality – that link to childhood and home. Surely that's why this meal looms large in the mind (and belly) of her son. Then again, it's grandpa's favourite, too. He slurps up a few mouthfuls before setting the bowl down and leaning back in his rocking chair, fly swatter in one hand, unlit cigarette in the other. His grandson plays on the floor beside him.

In Chinese, there are various sayings to describe the happiness of old age. One is 'er sun rao xi' (儿孙绕膝), which refers to the pleasure of children and grandchildren playing around your knees; another is 'si shi tong tang' (四世同堂) – four generations under one roof.

Shi returns studiously to her shoemaking without having eaten a bite, despite all that work. 'Personally, I don't like this dish – it's too sweet,' she says, half to herself, as the rhythmic whirr of the sewing machine fills the yard once again.

SHI FUMEI'S CHEESE AND HOME SWEET HOMECOMING

施孃火腿烩乳饼

SERVES 4–6

I asked for the Chinese name of this dish, but Shi couldn't give me one. I'll simply call it 施孃火腿烩乳饼 (Shi's braised ham and cheese).

440g fresh Dali cheese, sliced 1cm thick, 5cm long and 3cm wide

½ cup shaved brown sugar (or replace with ¼ cup brown sugar)

120g ham, half fat half lean, thinly sliced to match the shape of the cheese

1 cup fermented sweet rice (available jarred in Chinese supermarkets)

2 eggs, beaten lightly

1 cup canola oil

Heat oil over high heat in a wok, fry cheese pieces a few seconds on each side until golden. Remove from oil and put aside.

Scoop up excess oil but leave a spoonful in the wok; add ham to wok, stir until fat is released, scoop up ham and put aside.

Add 2 tbsp oil to wok over high heat, add fermented rice, stir a few times; add previously cooked cheese and ham, as well as the sugar, stir rapidly a few times; add eggs and stir for a minute; scoop into a bowl.

Put the mix in a steamer, steam on high heat for 15 minutes.

Serve hot with rice.

THE CARAVAN COMES TO SHAXI

THE FIRST time I visited Shaxi was back in 2003. I wanted to hike on the famed caravan route, and Shaxi was where my local guides brought me. Back then, the entrance to the village was a bustling weekly bazaar where Yi people from the mountains would come to sell their walnuts, honey and mushrooms, and buy some farm tools or maybe a pair of high heels for the girls.

I seemed to be the only traveller that day. I wandered around the village, poking my head into beautiful courtyards to find large bamboo trays of drying mushrooms or chrysanthemum flowers. And then I reached the market square, shaded by centuries-old Chinese scholar trees and encircled by beautiful merchant houses crafted from timber and tamped earth. A magnificent open-air stage, with intricately carved flying eaves and cornices, opened on to the square.

But something was clearly afoot. The village square was half dug up, stones piled in heaps everywhere. A massive renovation was underway. I wandered into the 600-year-old Xingjiao Temple opposite the opera stage to find the source of the commotion – a conservation team of Chinese staff and carpenters that had made a makeshift office in the side rooms of the temple. Dr Jacques P. Feiner was leading the operation.

The fact that Sideng Street, the heart of Shaxi, survives in its original state is down to an international effort that began in 2001, spearheaded by Jacques, a Swiss academic and restoration expert from the Swiss Federal Institute of Technology. It's no exaggeration to say that his efforts – and a lucky case of 'right place, right time', kick-started the effort to keep this historic town from wholesale redevelopment. Working with the World Monuments Fund (WMF), the Shaxi government and enthusiastic local residents, Jacques and his team helped preserve this historic jewel.

Jacques came to China in 2001. The first time he saw the town and the village square he instantly knew it was something special. It was badly rundown, and some of the courtyards had ten families living in them, but – critically – the courtyard houses, opera stage and historic temple had not been torn down. Jacques could feel the historic importance of Shaxi and the role it played as a market centre hundreds of years ago.

The Shaxi valley follows the line of the Heihui River through Jianchuan County,

a broad, fertile plain scattered with villages and farmsteads. A thousand years ago, when Dali was a mighty kingdom, this town was a thriving centre for trade. Later on, a proliferation of salt villages in the surrounding mountains made it a distribution hub for salt bound for northwest Yunnan and Tibet. Perhaps our Master's Well salt was once bought and sold in Shaxi's market square.

When the old trading routes ceased, however, and modern roads came to Yunnan, Shaxi was all but forgotten. One had to journey over winding, hilly lanes for thirty minutes to reach the village from the main road. It used to be a three-hour drive to either Lijiang in the north or Dali Old Town in the south, which was just far enough to keep sleepy Shaxi tourist-free for decades.

Still, Jacques was worried about Shaxi. In China, development – when it comes – happens so fast that the risk of destruction is very high. After encountering Shaxi, Jacques sought out local officials. 'You really have a big chance here,' he told them. But no one believed him.

Jacques had been working on heritage protection in Yemen before he came to China. During a meeting with the WMF in New York, they told him they were keen to find projects in China and asked him for advice. When Jacques showed them pictures of Shaxi, they were very excited. At the time, WMF was putting together a list of the '100 Most Endangered Monuments', and they suggested that Jacques nominate Shaxi to be on the list. Working with Chinese colleagues, Jacques completed the application for the endangered monuments list. In 2002, it was accepted.

'What was incredible was the impact the nomination had. For the Chinese it was a really big thing, as it was for us. It made people look at Shaxi differently. They organised a huge conference with about one hundred journalists in Kunming to announce that it had made the list,' Jacques recalled.

Jianchuan County had already contributed USD 40,000 for the planning work. The Swiss Development Corporation agreed to match that, and this money paid for flights for foreign specialists to come in and conduct surveys. In six months they had a rehabilitation plan. WMF provided around USD 400,000. The Chinese government matched that amount. Private sponsors also chipped in. 'From a small snowball we got something like an avalanche,' Jacques said.

By June 2002, renovation work was ready to start. The first stages of planning were extremely difficult. Schemes were created on computers, but the Shaxi valley didn't have a constant supply of electricity, so power cuts were common. Swiss and local Yunnan architects and engineers used different design software, making

communication and collaboration a real challenge. During the summer, all it did was rain.

But the biggest challenge of all was that the Chinese and the Swiss differed in their approaches to conservation. Local decision-makers wanted to replace everything and build it new. They insisted on rebuilding, but Jacques told them it was against the charter of WMF. 'We had these debates many times. This is not just a Shaxi issue; instead, this is common when collaboration on conservation is involved,' Jacques said.

Fortunately, in the beginning of 2003, a man named Huang Yingwu joined the project. He was an exchange student from Nanjing, just finishing his studies in Switzerland. In the beginning, he was only looking for something part time, but soon he became completely fascinated by Shaxi and the vision of developing it in what Jacques calls 'a soft and tender way'. Huang took over the role of on-site architect and manager.

Jacques's team pledged to replace only wood that had rotted or was beyond repair. 'For me, restoration is about the value of an original,' Jacques says. 'Why do we only try to touch up a grand master, and not repaint it? This was always the big issue for us. What is an original and what is a copy? Something with real age, you can feel it. It has imperfections and this gives it a special ambience. If you replace it, all you are left with is a ghost of the original.'

Jacques tried to stop any expansion or changes that he felt would destroy Shaxi.

He told me, 'I remember when an investor came to town and wanted to build a big hotel in the middle of the rice paddy fields by the Heihui River, which would block the most beautiful view from Sideng Street. On the one hand this represented money and investment for Shaxi, but on the other hand it would have destroyed one of Shaxi's main assets – the unique landscape.'

After five years, the rehabilitation project was complete. It was time for Jacques to leave. 'I had given what I could, and with Huang Yingwu and the local team in charge, the project was in good hands,' Jacques recalled. 'Shaxi was in a position to run by itself.' Still, leaving Shaxi did hurt. 'My current office is full of pictures of Shaxi,' Jacques admitted.

Now, twelve years since my last trip here, we park the car and I enter the village with some anxiety. To my immediate relief, I discover that the temple, the opera stage and the old winding lanes are all still intact. Even the original cobblestones, polished by centuries of foot traffic, have been meticulously put back into place on the square.

Many of my old friends are still there, and a number of them have built lodges or businesses capitalising on the boom. Huang Yingwu still lives in the village and continues to advise the local government on conservation and development. He is the unofficial spokesperson for Shaxi. I catch up with Huang to ask if he's happy with where Shaxi is today.

'I can't say whether I am happy or unhappy with where Shaxi is. I am just constantly curious about where Shaxi will be next, and I try my best to positively influence its development,' he says. Huang has come to understand that restoring the physical buildings was actually the easy part. What's been hardest is trying to develop Shaxi in a way that helps to mend the torn social fabric. Many local villagers have rented out their homes and moved out of the village square. 'They might have more money, but are they living a better life?' Huang asks. Fortunately, he says that the current county governor understands the value of Shaxi, and that makes a huge difference.

I go out for a walk in the evening, just as the sun starts to dip behind the old opera stage. The day-trippers are gone, and calm has returned. Out by Heihui River, a young man urges horses carrying firewood on their backs across a stone bridge. The shadows of trees are long on the cobbled path. It's almost possible to imagine the old Shaxi, to hear the tinkling bells of passing horse caravans, the shouts from the stage, the calls of sellers at the market.

I know what Jacques means. You can feel, deep down, when something has real age and history.

CRASHING A BAI WEDDING

BUTTERY YELLOW rapeseed flowers carpet the fields around Shaxi. Their fragrance fills the air as I lace up my shoes and go out for a morning run. It's 10:00 a.m. on a Sunday, our third day in Shaxi, and the fields are quiet. Where is everybody? Most farmers in the countryside don't go by weekly calendars, and they certainly don't rest on Sundays.

I brush aside the thought and continue on my way. Several Bai ladies, dressed in pristine blue dresses and carrying loaded baskets on their backs, cross the path ahead of me, clearly heading somewhere important. One of them momentarily sets her heavy basket on the railing of the stone bridge to rest, and I enquire as I pass by. It turns out they are on their way to a wedding.

They say it's at a village called 'Xiang Shang', or at least that's how it sounds to me. Bai people in this area don't speak the Yunnan dialect that I am familiar with. Wherever the wedding is, I am determined to find out. I'm curious to see how things have changed, and, being a fellow Yunnan girl, I'm sure the family won't mind one more well-wisher crashing their party.

A few inquiries later, the wedding location has been clarified and I know it's due to start in the late afternoon. I reassemble my team a few hours later to set up an ambush where I know the wedding party will pass on its way to deliver the bride to the groom's family home.

Suddenly the wedding party blasts its way into view, announcing its arrival with deafening firecrackers. A rag-tag motorcade of vehicles pulls up, headed by a red convertible garlanded in flowers.

About two dozen young people including the bride and groom colonise the roundabout, where there is a newly erected bronze statue depicting the ancient caravan road - a 'muleteer', life-sized, leading a trio of horses, and a bit of mild-mannered hazing ensues. All the parents, older relations and in-laws have gone ahead to the house of the groom's family. This is a ritual for the young (no one seems older than 21), and they take to it with gusto. The bride, a pretty, dark-skinned girl in a white wedding dress and veil, feigns indignation as a boy in a purple sweater tries to goad her into kissing the groom. The groom, looking especially young and fresh-faced in his suit, half-heartedly makes to kiss her . . . until she storms off in

her high heels, a smile on her face. Someone yells and the wedding party rolls out, mostly on foot this time, as the village is only about a kilometre away.

I offer my regards to the groom and he signals for us to follow along. We step in with the procession, cars crawling beside us at walking pace. A young boy wearing an oversized rucksack packed to the brim with explosives lights a bundle of firecrackers every minute or so, tossing them into ploughed fields beside the road where the soft earth barely cushions their machine gun explosions. I glean from friends of the couple that the bride and groom are childhood sweethearts, meaning this is not an arranged marriage. We turn on to a dusty lane that leads into the village where the groom's family lives. The firecrackers build to a crescendo as the groom dutifully carries his bride piggyback the last few steps through the gate to his family home.

According to British anthropologist C. P. Fitzgerald, who wrote a study of Bai culture entitled *The Tower of Five Glories*, wealthy Bai families used to pay to have the bride conveyed to the groom's family home in a covered sedan chair. If several weddings happened to be taking place in the same area on the same auspicious day, it was not unheard of for the sedan chairs to get mixed up and brought to the wrong house. Since the weddings were arranged, and the brides and grooms unacquainted, it was only when the parents of the bride arrived later to greet their new son-in-law that they would realise he had been eagerly consummating his marriage not to their daughter but to a total stranger. You can imagine this would have been rather awkward for all parties involved. So, writes Fitzgerald, the practice of a covered sedan chair was quietly scrapped in favour of one where the bride was clearly visible.

At this wedding, there is a bustle of activity in the front yard of the groom's house. Neighbours and family members old and young admire the bride's dowry, displayed proudly under the eaves of the two-storey house. The dowry includes a refrigerator and an air conditioner, still packaged in their cardboard delivery boxes. Freshly painted furniture holds stacks of duvets, crisp new sheets and blankets wrapped in ribbons. A new motorbike, a machine for milling pig feed, sacks of grain, clothes, slippers, cushions, rolls of toilet paper and embroidered wall-hangings make up the rest.

I can't help but marvel at the thoughtfulness and practicality of the dowry. Seeing it all stacked together like this, shiny and new, must be like seeing one's future laid out in objects. Everything a young Bai couple needs to make a life together. I think back to Shi Fumei, stitching shoes with the sewing machine that came as part of her dowry twenty years earlier.

When my parents got married, there was no dowry because everyone was poor.

At my parents' wedding, my father and mother received thirty hot water thermoses, I was told, the common red metal type printed with a Chinese character for double happiness or a pairing of male and female ducks. In those days it was considered a practical wedding gift. But thirty?

A group of children marvel at one dowry item in particular: a silver and pink picture frame holding a hundred 100 RMB bills in neat, overlapping rows. 'How much is in there?' I ask. 'Ten thousand yuan!' someone yells. 'Are they real?' My question is rewarded with looks of disdain. Of course they are!

I walk past small clusters of guests to offer my red envelope of wedding money to the groom; he shakes his head to refuse politely. The young man next to him, playing the role of best man, points me toward a desk behind the pile of duvets and sheets. I should have looked first. This is the formal wedding registry. Two older family members enter details in a notebook: amount, giver's name, relationship to the couple. Most people offer 200 to 500 RMB. In due time, the couple will reciprocate by giving the same or more at other weddings.

I make my contribution to the couple's future and get ready to join the meal. The newlyweds will move in to this house; two rooms have already been cleared for them. In Bai culture, the bride generally lives with the groom's family. I learn that the groom's family has two daughters who have already married and live elsewhere.

C. P. Fitzgerald also notes about the Bai culture that, 'where ancestor worship plays a major role it is natural that the bearing of children, especially sons, should be considered the first duty of women and the principal object of marriage.'

This sounds to me exactly like any traditional Chinese family. I remember my grandma telling me stories of when she gave birth to her second daughter during the Sino-Japanese War. She wasn't permitted to rest or even eat eggs (which were then considered an important nutrition supplement for women who just gave birth). My grandfather would have divorced her if she hadn't given birth to my father on the third try. It is the son that carries the family name and traditionally looks after parents in their old age.

The yard is filling up. Guests pass around warm bowls of ginger tea with popped rice floating in it. It starts to drizzle and the crowd moves closer to the house, nibbling on peanuts and sunflower seeds. The elders sit resplendently in the main living room, their senior status affording them the best seats.

The bride re-emerges after a wardrobe change. Her white wedding gown, a sure sign of western influence, has now been replaced with a bright red traditional

Chinese wedding dress, elaborately embroidered with a phoenix.

Then dinner happens, and what a show it is. Low tables with bench seats are squeezed into every spare bit of yard. Even so, there are too many guests, so guests take turns eating. It's remarkably efficient and well organised. We eat in the second shift. The leftovers from the first serving are briskly removed and a new plastic tablecloth is laid down, ready to be covered with stir-fried pork and chillies, spicy fish, rice noodles and big chewy hunks of tofu.

This is the familiar *ba da wan* (八大碗), or Eight Big Bowls, a standard set menu reserved for important Bai occasions. It's a tribute to the brilliance of rural hospitality; everything is cooked and served from enormous woks in one corner of the yard. Friends and relatives help with the cooking, serving and washing up, and it seems like the whole of Shaxi has been invited. People from all walks of life are here, some dressed in fine wedding clothes, others in worn work attire. Children, parents, teenagers and the elderly.

Once again, I am reminded of the similarities between births, weddings and funerals in China. Each occasion calls for a gathering of friends and family for a big feast. The guests simply chatter merrily about neighbours, relatives and local politics; no particular speech about the newlyweds or the deceased is offered. For each occasion, the point – whether in shared joyfulness or tearful solidarity – is simply to show up as a part of the community.

XIAGUAN AND
WEISHAN COUNTY

BEYOND THE BAI

ALL THE non-Bai people in Dali seem to congregate in Xiaguan, the new capital of Dali Prefecture. While it's only 12 kilometres south of the old town, Xiaguan, culturally speaking, may as well be as far away as the provincial capital of Kunming.

Life in Xiaguan in the 1970s was raw. Ghost stories and death were all around. I grew up in a hydro power station construction community by the Xi'er River at the very edge of the city. Kids were not allowed near the river because a young girl had drowned there, caught by a river ghost. Loud music often floated over from across the river – yet another funeral procession. We were exposed to death as naturally as we were exposed to the wind.

To me, Bai people, and especially the women, always seemed beautiful and romantic. They wore flowers on their dresses and lived in bright white houses around Erhai Lake. In comparison, the mountain-dwelling Yi people were mysterious and distant. No physical walls separated our hillside Chinese workers' community from the Yi or the Bai, but we had little contact. It was a different way of life.

One more thing we were forbidden to do as kids was wander too high up the mountain. This was because the Luoluo people would steal us, or so we were told. I came across the word 'Luoluo' again several decades later, reading Quentin Roosevelt's writing from the 1920s. Like the Han Chinese in Yunnan, he too referred to the mountainous Yi ethnic group as 'Luoluo', a derogatory word that conjured up the image of dark-skinned people with wild eyes, high cheekbones and rough hands, carrying bushels of corn by means of wide hemp straps around their foreheads.

At the hydro power station, workers were usually very young when they started – often barely teenagers. They referred to themselves by the year that they joined, so my father was a '63. They were mostly youngsters from other parts of Yunnan, arriving in Xiaguan on the backs of trucks, ready to carry 100-kilogram electricity poles on their young shoulders.

The workers built simple houses of woven bamboo on the slopes of the Cangshan Mountains. The walls were covered with newsprint, the wallpaper of that time, so one could simultaneously lie in bed and read up on Mao Zedong's latest speech.

Unlike Dali Old Town, which was contained by a rectangular wall and lined with cobblestone streets, Xiaguan boasted taller buildings – some three stories high! Xiaguan proper, a 2-kilometre walk from our mountain community, meant modern things like soda pop and movies. That was where you went to buy meat on Sundays, or to catch the bus to the outside world. That was where you went if you got hurt badly or were seriously ill.

These days Xiaguan is sprawling outwards around the southern and eastern shore of the lake, rendering unrecognisable the sleepy provincial town I remember from my childhood. Fancy villas and apartments line the landscaped highway. Everybody wants to be by the water, it seems.

I am eager to see the changes my childhood neighbourhood has gone through. Together with my brother, I've arranged to visit our old neighbour who still lives there.

A RIVER OF MEMORY

IT IS with a mix of excitement and trepidation that my brother and I, ever shrinking leg of ham in tow, make our way back to the hillside featured in my earliest memories.

The Xi'er River drains from Erhai Lake at the southwest pass of the Dali valley, where the water runs high and fast. My parents came here to harness the power of the water as part of the construction team that built the Xi'er River Hydro Electric Power Plant, a series of four stations gating the river. The one in front of the hillside where I grew up is Stage Number One, and stages Two, Three and Four are just a few kilometres apart, further down the river to the west.

We left Xiaguan in 1981 as the plant neared completion. I was 10 years old. Around 10000 construction workers were leaving at that time, moving on to other projects like the Manwan Power Plant in the south of the province, or the Lubuge Power Plant in the east.

The most skilled workers were often invited to embark on more lucrative and exotic missions overseas. My father considered going to Cameroon in the late 1970s, but decided that my brothers and I were still too little. To give us a better education, he worked his *guanxi* – his connections – as an electrician to relocate us to the provincial capital, Kunming. Better to get a superior education than more money, my father believed. I greatly benefited from his decision.

At that time, our neighbour, whom we called Uncle Yang, was approaching retirement age (50 in those days), so he stayed on in Xiaguan. His current house was built in 1984, part of a row of single-storey brick homes that constituted the first solid chunk of real estate on the hillside. Before that, we had all lived in temporary homes on the same plot – shacks, really, made of bamboo.

The first thing I am struck by upon my return is how much the view has changed. 'None of these buildings existed then,' says Uncle Yang, waving his arm in an arc that encompasses roads, apartments and the hulking high-rises in the distance. In my childhood memories, there was only the river and the Bai villages across the river, and nothing but mountains further along.

The Xi'er River is now ringed by two broad highways, and the incessant groan of trucks drowns out the sound of rushing water. Progress has brought industry, noise and commerce. But despite all that, Uncle Yang and his family have made this forgotten corner of Xiaguan their own. He proudly shows us his vegetable plot, arranged on the steep terraces. Pipes running this way and that distribute wastewater from his house to a pool used to irrigate the beds. It's organically fertilised, too, with all the neighbours 'contributing' via an outhouse in the middle of the field.

'We plant a little bit of everything so we can eat something different every day,' he says. Whatever they can't eat, they share with the neighbours. Uncle Yang grew up in the countryside, so growing things comes naturally.

As we speak, an elderly neighbour picks her way down the steep path to the vegetable plot and calls out enthusiastically, 'You should come here and see the garden in August and September – everything's green!'

I help Uncle Yang pick some fava beans and garlic scapes from his plot. 'You are about twenty days early for my cherries,' he says regretfully. Small in stature and neatly dressed, Uncle Yang is jolly and playful; he treats me like a niece, even though we're not blood relations.

Uncle Yang takes my arm and points out a patch of scrub ground a few metres beyond his onion patch. 'That's where your house was.' My brother perks up. 'You know, I remember playing outside the house, by a willow tree.' I also remember that tree. We used to take willowy branches and weave them into wreathes in the summer, like those worn by Olympic athletes.

The sky threatens rain, so we move inside. Yang's home is neat and organised. Tools and utensils all have their own spots on the wall within convenient reach. A homemade rice scoop – 'the perfect shape,' Uncle Yang points out – sits in the rice box in the porch area. He scoops out one portion of white rice, one portion of millet and one portion of cornmeal, mixing them together for the rice cooker. This nutritious, organic mix is enough to make any whole food devotee green with envy.

A widescreen television dominates the small living room. There is a bowl of orange plums with velvety skins on the table. Calendars are neatly and symmetrically hung, the days crossed off in pen. There is a fish tank with a few goldfish and multi-coloured stones on the bottom. In the master bedroom the walls are adorned with black and white photographs of Yang's wife dressed in Western clothing. The photos hark back to a time when a trip to a photo studio was a special occasion.

I bring from the car a chunk of our ham along with two bottles of glucosamine pills that I brought from the United States. It's hard to think of an appropriate gift, but my father advised me that Yang's wife has knee problems and glucosamine helps.

She puts the bottles aside with a big smile and tells me, 'Think of this as your

own home. You shouldn't be bringing presents when you come home.' Medicine, she appreciates; ham, no. 'No need to bring ham, we have our own. We will use our ham,' she says, drawing open a cloth curtain in the corner of the kitchen to reveal a small rack of drying ham, sausages and bacon.

Yang takes us to his tiny bathroom and lifts the cover from the washbasin to reveal fish and shrimp swimming around. They will also feature in our meal. He then shows us the innovative wastewater system he has attached to his washing machine. A moveable set of pipes lets Yang channel water from the first, soapy load into the drain, and the second and third loads to the garden plot outside.

On low stools, we set to work on Yang's porch, popping fava beans out of their shells. Inside, his wife and their eldest daughter fry tiny shrimp whole in the wok. The sizzle of the oil mixes with the rhythmic plop of our beans into a bowl, and the occasional faint honk of trucks on the highway.

As we work, I ask him what would happen if the government wanted to develop the land where he lives. He is pragmatic. 'If people want this land, then the government will have to take care of us and find us new housing. But who would be interested in it? I'm happy to stay here forever; we've made a good home.' He reaches down for another handful of fava beans.

Back in the kitchen, Uncle Yang mixes the shelled fava beans in an enamel bowl with a heap of sticky rice flour and a spoonful of salt. He adds just the right amount of water and starts forming irregular-shaped cakes that resemble pistachio-studded Turkish delight. These he fries until golden, and we munch on them as a pre-dinner snack. The dish is called *qingwa bei shiban*, a silly name buried deep in my memories. It means 'frogs carrying slate stones'.

The smell of Uncle Yang's ham soon fills the air. In the small room, the aroma is chokingly rich, almost sickly, but it's soon tempered by freshly plucked garlic scapes, which join the ham in the wok. One dish complete, Yang's wife starts the next one by taking strips of *rushan* (乳扇) (paper-thin fans of dried cheese, another Bai dairy specialty), and dropping them into the oil where they expand and bubble dramatically, transforming into crunchy sheets. With just a single burner and wok, one dish is cooked after the other, so only the last couple dishes are still warm when we finally sit down to eat.

Figure skaters twirl in sequined outfits on the big screen TV as we feast on fish, chicken, shrimp, ham, fresh vegetables and the healthy grain medley. Before eating, our host performs one last pre-meal ritual. At his wife's reminder, he pops into the bedroom to take his insulin.

We reminisce about the old days. Yang explains how he met his wife in 1963 when she started working at the company. He's also a '63, same as my father. Uncle Yang and his wife recall how, as neighbours, everyone knew each other's business because only thin bamboo walls separated the workers' families. Their wedding was a simple affair, Uncle Yang's wife tells us. They shared a dinner and then pushed their beds together. Both worked for the construction company; he was an electrician and supervisor of the hydro plant switchboard, she a telephone operator. My mother was also an operator. She was 32 when she died. Out of respect, Uncle Yang doesn't like to mention her.

They both seem happy with their routines. Uncle Yang wakes up, spends two hours tending his vegetable plot, makes lunch, and then goes to the park to play chess. 'Sometimes he wins the grand prize in the senior competition,' his wife says proudly. The prize is 100 *yuan*, which at least pays rent for the month. After chess, Yang walks home, makes dinner and watches TV. 'The same every day,' he says contentedly.

Yang's wife loves to travel, and has a trip planned to Hong Kong soon. Uncle Yang can't go with her on account of his bad foot, she explains, which seems like a convenient arrangement for both of them. It's funny to observe Uncle Yang, previously so talkative in his vegetable plot, fall silent when sitting beside his wife. My dad tells me later that it's always like this. 'He's a retired soldier and country farmer; she's a tough-talking woman from Xiaguan.' I guess we know who wears the pants in this relationship.

The ham dish is nostalgia on a plate, just how my father used to cook it. But Yang's wife has been too hospitable; the dish turned out overly salty because she used too generous a ratio of ham to vegetables. It makes me think how tidbits of whatever you love are always tastier than a full plate. You can have too much of a good thing. Even ham.

After eating, Yang says he wants to take me for a walk. He leads the way nimbly down the steep hillside. We walk single file up the dusty highway above the river, hugging the embankment as heavily loaded trucks roar past us. The hydro plant comes into view, a row of blue buildings and a chained guard dog that barks at us half-heartedly. Uncle Yang trots further up the road and we stop at a bridge, once the sole path across the Xi'er River and the only access point into the old Kingdom of Dali from the south.

The bridge, *Tian Sheng Qiao*, or 'Naturally Born Bridge', is actually a single

boulder in the middle of the river that provides a fortuitous bridging point. We cross it tentatively, watching the water strike the rocks below in the fading light. According to legend, the bridge was the site of a battle in the Third century. Zhuge Liang, a famous strategist, captured the tribal leader Meng Huo seven times in succession, until Meng finally agreed to peace. Uncle Yang explains that the phrase 'qi qin meng huo' (七擒孟获) is still widely used to describe winning the heart of your opponent by strategy.

It's dark now, and after a moment's reflection we start back toward Uncle Yang's house. I can tell that this bridge means something to him. He seems happy, in his quiet way, that this spot near his home has a place in history.

STIR-FRIED HAM WITH GARLIC SCAPES

火腿炒蒜苔

SERVES 4–6

This is a classic stir-fry ham dish in Yunnan. Garlic scapes, the newly flowering stem of a garlic plant, are just one form of garlic used in Yunnan cuisine. The most common form is the bulbous root common also in Western cooking, which we call *da suan* (大蒜), or 'big garlic'. When garlic sprouts have grown to a height of 30 centimetres we often harvest them, leaving the bulb underground to sprout again. This we call *qing suan* (青蒜) or *suan miao* (蒜苗), 'garlic sprouts'. When the plant develops a flower bud, we harvest the stem before the flower opens. This we call *suan tai* (蒜苔), or garlic scapes. It's important to discard the older, tougher parts of the stem, and the best way to identify the edible portion is to use the nails of your index finger and thumb to pinch the stem. If you can successfully break a piece off without first breaking your nails, that's a tender part. Anything you can't break with your fingernails shouldn't be presented to your teeth!

200g ham, half lean and half fat, thinly sliced

300g garlic scapes, tender parts cut into 3cm-long pieces, other parts discarded

10 dried chilli peppers, whole or cut into 3cm pieces for a stronger flavour (optional)

2 tbsp canola oil

Add oil to wok over high heat until a little smoke rises from the wok; add fatty ham and cook until fat is released, then add dried chilli peppers and lean ham; stir for 1 minute, scoop into a bowl and set aside. Drain oil back into the wok.

Keep remaining oil in wok over high heat, add garlic scapes, stir vigorously for 1 minute; add back the cooked ham and chilli; stir and mix evenly.

Place on a plate or in a bowl; serve at room temperature.

FROGS CARRYING SLATE STONES

青蛙背石板

SERVES 4–6

Fresh fava beans are on everyone's dinner table in Yunnan and other southern provinces in China from January to March, but they are seldom used for cooking in northern China. A few years ago I found them at a farmers' market in Santa Monica, California, only slightly longer than the ones back home in Yunnan. Now I occasionally find them at the Chinese supermarket in the US or at specialty grocery stores. Few shoppers pick them up because few people know what to do with them. That said, they are common in middle eastern cooking.

Here is Uncle Yang's simple recipe.

1kg fresh fava beans, in pods

2 cups glutinous rice flour

2 tsp salt

1 cup canola oil

1 cup hot water

Peel off the outer green jackets and inner shells of the fava beans; separate each bean into two halves and place in a bowl.

Add glutinous rice flour, water and salt (to taste) to the bowl; knead for a few minutes until mixture becomes doughy. Cut into fist-sized chunks, shape into balls; place on a cutting board and cut the dough into slices. Sprinkle some dried rice flour over them and lay them out on a plate. This will prevent them from sticking together.

Add oil to a frying pan or wok over medium heat. Add rice-bean pieces to pan (as many pieces as fit comfortably in one layer), fry until golden and bubbling around the edges. Turn each piece and fry the other side until golden.

Remove from heat, place on a paper towel-lined plate to drain and cover tops with paper towels to remove excess oil. Repeat frying process with remaining pieces. Serve while hot. This dish does not taste good when cold, as the glutinous rice cakes harden as they cool.

WEISHAN

I FIRST visited the old town of Weishan in 2005 when I was planning to write a cookbook about authentic Chinese food, documenting the simple yet tasty cooking methods of my relatives in Yunnan. Weishan was the place to go, my uncle told me, and the town didn't disappoint.

The town is centred along a pedestrian street 2.5 kilometres long. It seems like everyone in town is a foodie, and everyone offers his or her expert advice about food. Eggplants are not as tasty after the summer rain; the best time to buy bacon is around 21 December. Even honey has a particular harvest time – one week! – also in December. Weishan is all about food.

In 2011, government officials in Weishan launched an annual Weishan Snack Festival, featuring local foods from all around the county. The festival is held on 8 February (lunar calendar) on a pedestrian street filled with snack stalls selling noodle salads, coloured rice balls, a local version of a buckwheat pancake and many other small local goodies.

This makes Weishan a must-visit destination for my ham quest.

A PLACE FORGED BY FIRE

WEISHAN YI and Hui Autonomous County is next door to Dali Old Town. Whereas Dali is Bai, Weishan is home mostly to Yi and Hui ethnic groups. Both powerfully independent in their own way, it means that even today Weishan stands slightly apart from Dali.

The Yi are also descendants of the powerful Nanzhao king Pi Luo Ge, whose rise to power in the early eighth century is well documented in various legends. The fire of Song Ming Lou occurred in Weishan. Upon uniting the kingdoms, Pi Luo Ge moved the capital of his kingdom to Dali Old Town, and Weishan faded into the background as the new kingdom thrived. Yet every 25 June (lunar calendar), the Yi in Weishan and around Yunnan commemorate the fire and Queen Bai Jie through celebrations of the Torch Festival.

In Weishan's old town today, all roads lead to Gongchen Tower, a once mighty Ming Dynasty gatehouse as wide as a dozen cars, with a red-beamed pavilion sitting atop it like a crown. The gatehouse presided over the town for more than 600 years. On 3 January, 2015, a fire ravaged the tower, rumoured to have originated from an electric stove in the teahouse on its second floor.

When we arrive three months later, restoration and rebuilding are underway. Elsewhere, too, it's clear that this ancient city is undergoing a makeover. Cobblestone roads are being updated, long lost street gates are being resurrected in freshly cut stone, shop fronts display touristic, period-style wooden signs, and even the street lights are now of a similar period style.

Fire brought the kingdom of Nanzhao into being; it built Weishan, and now it is taking the town in a different direction.

It's dark when we arrive at our guesthouse in Weishan's old town, having departed Uncle Yang's house after dinner. The streets are quiet, and flowers fill the open courtyard with the scent of spring.

The next morning, walking through Weishan's alleyways, I see an old lady selling incense and funerary goods. A cobbler works nearby in the open air. Two ladies hang noodles to dry in long, straight lines like curtains a little way down the street. A barbershop displays long-faded posters of hair models, as well as towels hung out to dry. There's the clack of mah-jong tiles from behind red wooden screens. And a few doors away is a little restaurant belonging to Qian Xingping.

I've known Chef Qian ever since my first visit to Weishan, and I've dined at his restaurant many times. Whenever I pass by, almost without fail I find him at the stove in his open kitchen, presiding over big white tin pots steaming with something delicious.

Together with his wife, Qian has operated the restaurant here since 1999, but the building itself is much older. It's a humble place. The walls are papered with posters advertising Dali beer, and the floor is bare concrete. It's dotted with a few mismatched tables and chairs. In the back there's more seating and an open yard with a flower garden. Beans are soaking in a bowl outside. Chunks of *larou* bacon, the same as those in Uncle Yang and Shi Fumei's houses, dangle from the ceiling, fat tapering off in opaque stalactites.

I ask Chef Qian if he could demonstrate a few dishes. He nods quietly and then returns to slicing and dicing with an enormous cleaver on a massive chopping block. 'It's from the trunk of a *shatan shu*,' he explains – confused by the accent I could only give my best guess that it's possibly beech wood. 'Soft, so that the wood doesn't dull the knife.' It's a present from a friend and he's used it for six years. They are hard to find now, he adds. On a corner, atop a large stove, a pot of *gutou tang* – pork bone stock – simmers away. A ladle of its milky-rich liquid is just an arm's reach away, ready to be poured into a sizzling wok to lend flavour and moisture.

Chef Qian proposes two ham dishes using *erkuai* (饵块), a specialty of Weishan. *Erkuai* is a type of cake made from rice that has been soaked, steamed, then pounded into a paste and kneaded. It has a gummy texture and can be served savoury or sweet, but I usually prefer it salty and spicy, Yunnan style. With the same ingredient and methods, but made into string-like noodles, it is called *ersi*. *Erkuai* comes in the shape of pancakes or bricks. *Erkuai* bricks last longer and are often sliced up for stir-fries, while *ersi* (饵丝) is often served in soup as an alternative to slippery

rice noodles, *mixian* (米线), or standard wheat noodles, *miantiao* (面条). The most famous Weishan noodle dish is called *parou ersi* (耙肉饵丝), a bowl of rice noodle soup topped with chunks of pork stewed so long that they melt in your mouth. *Shao erkuai* (烧饵块) is a popular local snack that employs *erkuai* as a pancake to wrap around pickles and chilli sauce like a Yunnanese burrito.

Our ham is down to half its original size. I present Chef Qian with a lean piece. He examines it, poking around with his fingers, and sniffs it expertly, almost like a sommelier with his wine. 'Pretty good ham,' he pronounces quietly. I am relieved.

The first dish is steamed ham inserted inside pieces of *erkuai*, sort of like a steamed ham sandwich. Brandishing his mighty cleaver, Chef Qian deftly slices the *erkuai* to size, slicing each piece neatly down the middle and inserting a sliver of ham. 'We eat this dish for festivals and celebrations,' he explains. After prepping the main ingredients, he pops out to the street for a cigarette and his wife takes over.

Their restaurant is named simply after the street it's on: South Street Restaurant (南街餐厅). Like many local restaurants, there is no menu. 'People just order what they want from whatever is displayed in the cabinet,' explains Qian. He particularly likes serving the local Yi people. 'Yi people come in from the mountains, and they always want a double portion of boiled meat, maybe with some salad, deep-fried stinky tofu and rice. They don't have much money to spend.' Local office workers have more money to splurge on elaborate dishes, he says. And then there's the out-of-town tourists.

'Even though they don't live here I still try hard to make them repeat customers. Word of mouth is the most powerful thing. Many travellers do come back.'

He goes on, 'My dishes, they're made with the simplest ingredients. If you use good ingredients and let the flavours shine, that's enough. Other restaurants try to make the dishes look more fancy. But I believe that sometimes people like a place just because they like a place – call it habit. I know which seats my regulars will sit in and what they like to order.'

Qian's wife calls us over. She is done with the preparation for another ham dish, this time a common stir-fry of *erkuai* pieces with fresh vegetables, dried chillies, and a pinch of a local spice called *caoguo* (草果) or Chinese cardamom. Chef Qian takes charge of the wok and spatula. Each ingredient is tossed into the wok at a precise moment to preserve its colour, bite and flavour. The cooking itself takes about a minute, which feels dizzyingly fast but results in a stunning display of colours.

Chef Qian lights another cigarette as he talks, sharing his food philosophy as we dig in. The rich sandwiches, with the smoky bite of our ham coming through perfectly against the neutral *erkuai*, are offset with a note of fresh chive.

Besides cooking at the restaurant, Chef Qian's favourite thing to do is to cater for large weddings and funerals in the countryside. He cooks al fresco, using enormous woks over wood fires. He shows us his travelling tools: giant utensils that he carries in a bamboo basket on his back, together with his mighty cleaver, chopping block and sharpening stone. 'The whole lot weighs 60 *jin* [30 kilograms], and each dish we make can serve 300 to 400 people,' he explains.

Chef Qian plans to continue cooking in Weishan until he retires. 'I want to improve the restaurant's environment and learn new skills like pickling and medicinal alcohols. Over time I want to innovate.'

When I ask what they might do after retirement, Qian's wife exclaims cheerfully, 'Whatever!' Then she adds, 'Well, I know what my husband would do. He likes to wander around the villages in the mountains, visiting the Yi folk up there. Their doors are never locked! If they are out he will just go inside and light a fire, have a drink and wait for their return.'

Chef Qian smiles shyly at the thought. 'Come join me to buy honey in the mountains on 21 December – just that week!'

CHEF QIAN'S FRIED ERKUAI (RICE CAKES) WITH HAM

火腿炒饵块

SERVES 4–6

100g ham, half lean and half fat, thinly sliced

300g *erkuai*, thinly sliced (or use *ersi* instead)

2 pieces Napa cabbage leaves, julienned into 2 cups

1 cup Chinese chives, cut into 3cm segments

2 cups snow pea vines, loosely packed

3 dried chilli peppers, torn by hand

2 tbsp mustard green pickle (see p136)

¼ cup canola oil

½ cup cooking broth (replace with water if necessary)

Salt, pepper, soy sauce, ground *caoguo*, a pinch or so to taste

Heat oil over high heat, add ham slices and cook until colour changes from red to dark brown.

Add Napa cabbage, stir evenly.

Add dried chilli pepper, rice cake. Stir evenly.

Add cooking broth, salt, soy sauce and *caoguo*, stir evenly.

Add chives and snow pea vine, stir quickly, adding a bit more water for moisture.

Add preserved vegetable, stir and mix. Remove from heat and transfer to a large plate. Serve hot.

CHEF QIAN'S HAM SANDWICHES

火腿蒸饵块

SERVES 4–6

250g *erkuai* brick

100g lean ham

10 sprigs of Chinese chives (use only the white stems), cut into 7cm segments

A few leaves of cilantro for garnish

Cut *erkuai* into 1cm thick, 7cm long, 3cm wide pieces; slice each piece open lengthways to the middle, being careful not to cut through to the other side. Each rice cake should consist of two ½cm-thick pieces connected lengthways on one side.

Slice ham thinly to matching shape – 7cm long and 3cm wide.

Place one piece of ham inside each opening of the rice cakes; arrange with opening side face down in a bowl, fanning out from the bowl's centre.

Put the bowl in a steamer, steam at high heat for 20 minutes.

Boil a cup of water, quickly blanch the chives, drain and refresh under cold water (this cools the chives and helps maintain their crisp green colour). Set aside for garnish.

Remove bowl from steamer, cover tightly with a plate and flip upside down so that the contents are on top of the plate.

Garnish with chives and cilantro, serve hot.

THE PICKLE LADY

AROUND THE corner from Chef Qian's eatery, we enter another courtyard to find Madame Chen Manhua. Madame Chen is 79 years old and she reigns over the most famous pickle 'empire' in Weishan, Yin Family Pickles (殷记咸菜). Despite her maiden name of Chen, she adopted her husband's name, Yin, for the company.

Madame Chen has a pickle recipe for every season. Winter is daikon radish and black beans; spring is garlic and garlic scapes; in the summer it's broad beans and string beans; autumn is for chillies and whole onions. All year round, Madame Chen sits in her covered courtyard with four family members and six other workers, everyone pickling. She has a persuasive way of talking and strong beliefs about her work.

'It's the quality that matters. Our pickles are hand made, which you can't rush. Machines cannot replace our work, either.' Madame Chen is multitasking, chatting as she patiently works on the garlic scapes, snipping away at the tough ends with a pair of scissors.

The aroma of the pickle workshop evokes memories of my childhood. My family, like most local families, didn't own a refrigerator until the mid-1990s. So preserving food was an essential part of everyday life. We cured ham and bacon if we slaughtered a pig, and we pickled vegetables after buying them in bulk at their cheapest.

The most common pickles in Yunnan are mustard greens, which are used almost every day to provide a spicy sour taste to stir-fried pork, potato or noodle soup. Daikon radish and beans (whole or ground) are also common; less so are chive roots, which perhaps is unsurprising given that they make for such pungently bad breath. The pickle possibilities are endless.

Yunnan pickles are often very salty, which helps them last longer, and also makes them excellent condiments for staples like rice. For manual labourers, a huge bowl of rice accompanied by a dose of pickles, all washed down with tea, makes for a low-cost but satisfying meal.

Growing up, my favourite Yunnan breakfast was a salty and spicy rice noodle soup. Pickles gave a sour and spicy kick to those steaming bowls of noodles. Years later, my uncle from Weishan gave me some Yin Family daikon pickles, packaged simply in plastic bags. To me, those strips of radish – covered in red chilli sauce, soured by pickling, then sweetened with sugar – were crunchy little mouthfuls of nostalgia.

All the hard work at Yin Family Pickles happens in the central courtyard. We arrive just as they are reconvening after a lunch break, during which Madame Chen also takes an hour-long nap. The staff cuts, washes and dries the vegetables. Behind the workers are rows and rows of metre-high jars, mostly filled to the brim with vegetables in pickling liquor, waiting to be sealed.

Madame Chen's youngest son takes us to the second floor of the courtyard's west wing to see the next phase of production: the pickling. Of course, this all happens inside sealed jars, so it just looks like a big storage room, but each jar is clearly labelled to identify its contents, be they beans or daikon. Every kind of pickle matures at a different rate, with some taking just a few days and some taking months. The wing opposite is the family's quarters; grandchildren loll on the sofa watching TV in the mid-afternoon. A couple of cats hide behind the flowerpots out front.

Madame Chen started her first business in the early 1970s. It was a secret, small-scale enterprise, selling fermented tofu on a little red table inside her house, only about 500 to 1000 pieces per year, with each piece selling for two cents. She got in trouble for it and had to shut down the business. Back then her entrepreneurial spirit was considered capitalist. Madame Chen subsequently got a position in a textile factory, but had to leave that job to take care of her four children. As China changed, she resumed her entrepreneurial activities and started making pickles again. Her pickles helped to subsidise the family's living.

'I used to pound chillies at night,' she recalls. 'That was hard work. My eyes would tear up from the spice. I set up a small woven bamboo table in front of my door with three jars of pickles: mustard greens, daikon and cabbage. I was so shy that I'd hide inside the house until someone hollered for pickles.'

Madame Chen tells me her story as she works. Her youngest daughter sits next to her, also trimming vegetables.

The turning point in Madame Chen's pickle business came with the birth of her second grandchild. She gave up her mobile pickle stand, sold the house they were living in, and moved into their current courtyard in 1999. Now, Yin Family Pickles is the largest pickle venture in town, and business is thriving. Eighty per cent are repeat customers,' she tells me.

'*Ziran lai, ziran lai,*' Madame Chen says often as she talks. If anything, this is the motto of Yin Family Pickles and of Madame Chen herself. It means: In time, things happen naturally. Don't rush them.

So for how long does she plan to keep making pickles? Her daughter chips in,

'We told her to stop but she won't!'

I ask her who she will pass the business on to when she retires, and it seems I've touched on a sore topic. She lowers her voice. 'My younger son, whom you've met, also works in the business. I would like to pass the business to him, but he is not very bright. He didn't like school, not much education. My elder son is very well educated, but he has an important government job.'

She sighs, and carries on clipping. I know better than to ask about passing the business to her daughters; girls won't continue the Yin family name.

Suddenly, the parrot hanging in the cage above the workers yells out, '*Ren ge zai? Mae xian cai!*' in the local Weishan dialect. The staff chuckle. It means, 'Anyone there? Sell pickles!' They bought the bird when he was a baby, three or four years ago. He's heard customers shouting 'anyone there?' so many times that he now repeats it perfectly.

Another love of Madame Chen's is travelling. She tells me that she recently went to Beijing, but the packaged tour food was awful. I suggest that she might take a selection of her pickles when she travels next to spice up her food.

'Certainly not! I've been looking at them for thirty years. I can't stand them anymore!'

PICKLED MUSTARD GREENS

酸腌菜

Madame Chen's workshop only makes pickles in large batches. For the benefit of people preparing this at home, I have taken this recipe from her son. Chinese people tend to cook by feel and experience, not by recipe, so the instructions are very approximate, such as requiring 'a few kilograms of vegetable' and adding 'a little bit of fennel seed'. For that reason I have used as guidance the proportions of a similar recipe from my aunt in Kunming, who is also an excellent cook. The end result is the recipe below. The only significant difference is that Madame Chen uses fennel seeds, while my aunt prefers ground star anise; both spices give the pickle a sweet, spicy taste.

This pickle is essential in Yunnan cooking. It is often used as a key ingredient in fried rice, noodle soups and fish or chicken stews to provide the spicy and sour taste that is so distinctive to Yunnan cuisine. Sometimes, it also serves as an accompaniment to congee.

Please note, it is extremely important that the entire process be kept grease-free. A slightly oily hand, chopstick or chopping board will ruin the pickle process, as the vegetable will turn mouldy and mushy in the jar. Remember as well that this is a multi-day process, as it requires one full day to dry the mustard leaves.

2.8kg mustard leaves, with stems

3 tbsp salt

a piece of ginger, the size of a thumb, julienned

1 tsp fennel seeds

Separate each mustard leaf, lay out under the sun or dry on a clothesline for one day; then rinse clean with water and cut into 1cm pieces.

Add leaves and salt to a large bowl (bowl should be thoroughly cleaned with dish detergent), use hands to mix thoroughly,

½ cup ground dried chilli pepper (optional, for a spicy Yunnan taste)

2 tbsp brown sugar

then let sit for half an hour to release liquid from the vegetable. After half an hour, use both hands to squeeze out the liquid. Place into another clean bowl. Discard the liquid.

Add ginger, fennel seeds, chilli pepper and brown sugar; mix thoroughly. Add more salt to taste.

Pack tightly into a pickle jar, preferably the type with a rim at the top for a tighter water seal. If not, just seal tightly to minimise exposure to air.

Let sit at room temperature for 3–5 days. When the green stems of the vegetable turn yellowish, they are ready to eat. Once ready, keep the jar inside the refrigerator. When dishing out a small portion for cooking, it's equally important to use grease-free utensils and reseal tightly after each use. This way, the pickles will keep for months.

DALI OLD TOWN

RETURN TO DALI

MY BROTHER drops us off at the gate of Dali Old Town to return to his day job in Kunming. The Old Town bans car traffic during the day because the streets are narrow, and there is already too much foot traffic. We drag our suitcases over the cobblestones in the direction of my house, but first we make a stop at the local noodle joint in front of the gate, a place called Liyuan Restaurant.

Liyuan (丽缘) is really a hole-in-the-wall noodle shop. It's 2 metres wide, 5 metres deep, and always busy. The lovely Bai husband and wife owners start work every day at 6:00 a.m. preparing the pork bone stock for soup. Then the wife cooks each bowl of noodles or fries each portion of rice over a four-burner gas cooker at the front of the shop. The husband busies himself in the back, preparing bundles of chives or washing dishes. They close whenever their day's supply sells out, usually between 3:00 and 5:00 p.m.

This time, like every time, they serve me with a smile. 'Hui lai la!?' they ask – 'You're back!?' The greeting makes me feel like I am home.

After returning to my house, I go to check how the plants are doing on the porch. I weed a little, and rearrange the cut flowers our housekeeper just brought back from the market. Everyone in Dali has a garden, as well as a few flowering camellia trees, big or small. At this time of the year, encouraged by the spring sun, the camellias are in full bloom, pink and white, the size of my palm.

I head out alone on my bike and cruise down Bo'ai Road for a cup of coffee at Bakery 88, a café run by a German lady who has been baking in Dali since 2007. Out on the street, a local farmer carries a basket on his back, yelling in a very low voice, 'Mae fengmi!' It takes me a moment to decipher that he is selling raw honey. There is a large clay jar inside the bamboo basket on his back, and he carries a few empty plastic bottles with him. He weighs the honey and pours it into a bottle for customers to take home. I smile. Dali hasn't changed.

FAITH, FLOWER, WEED AND FOOD

DALI HAS an irresistible allure to outsiders, a spirit that seems to draw in folks from different places and cultures.

Before the middle of the nineteenth century, very few westerners had set foot in China's interior, and even fewer had made it as far as Yunnan Province, kept out by the impenetrable mountains of Sichuan and Guizhou. Even Chinese living in the eastern part of the country as recently as the Ming Dynasty (1368--1644) would have had little concrete notion of Yunnan's geography. My ancestors, like most Han Chinese in Yunnan, were sent there by the Emperor in the Ming Dynasty, either as prisoners or soldiers. They settled the 'barbaric land'.

Many of the first westerners to make it to Yunnan had two goals in mind: faith and flowers. Missionaries and botanists (often they were both) were among the first wave of foreigners to record their adventures. One such arrival, a French Catholic missionary and plant collector named Father Jean Marie Delavay (1834–1895), lived for nearly ten years in Dali, collecting specimens in the region between Dali and Lijiang, and discovering thousands of new species of plants. He was the first to document the diverse flora and fauna on the rocky slopes of the Cangshan Mountains. The Latin suffix *delavayi* is applied to plants that were introduced to the West by Delavay, almost all from Yunnan.

Father Delavay's Yunnan adventures were influenced by another naturalist, Father Armand David (1826–1900). Father David shed even more light on the botanical wonders of Yunnan and China in the 1880s, gathering thousands of specimens, many of which were new to science, including thirteen new species of rhododendron. Also an accomplished zoologist, Father David documented a number of wild animals hitherto unknown to science. Most remarkable of all, Father David still found time to be a missionary between his scientific pursuits, and a diligently devoted one at that.

These botanical explorations carried with them considerable risk in the wilds of Yunnan. George Forrest, a Scotsman and professional botanist, made his first expedition to Yunnan in 1904, setting up his base of operations in Dali. On an expedition close to the Tibet border, his adventures took an unexpected turn when a group of Tibetan lamas set upon his party. Forrest was fortunate to get away. Other plant hunters, including a French missionary named Jean Andre Soulie, contended with similar challenges and were not as lucky. These incidents didn't deter Forrest, however, who made six more expeditions to Yunnan, discovering scores of species new to Western science. He had a genuine affection for the local Bai people, too, helping to inoculate thousands of Dali residents against smallpox at his own expense.

One of Yunnan's larger-than-life itinerant foreigners was Joseph Rock, an eccentric Austro-American explorer and botanist who lived for many years in the mountains near Lijiang, writing the history of the Naxi people (a local ethnic community in the Lijiang area). Rock was legendarily extravagant. He would embark on his adventures with a huge entourage of Naxi servants, and he would bring along every portable luxury, including a collapsible bathtub. A self-styled buccaneer, he reportedly carried a pair of Colt 45 pistols under his waistcoat.

By the 1930s and 1940s, with the invasion of China by Japan, men like Rock struggled to continue their lives in China's southwest. Yunnan became a battleground; the Japanese bombed the province, and the British and Americans battled to open Burma Road. Rock held on until the founding of the People's Republic of China in 1949. Faced with the prospect of leaving the picturesque village where he had made his home, he wrote, 'I want to die among those beautiful mountains rather than in a bleak hospital bed all alone.' Despite his best efforts, Rock never returned to China.

Yunnan was then swept along with the rest of China through the decades that followed. Foreigners began travelling to Yunnan again in large numbers starting from the mid-1980s; the city hasn't looked back since.

POTATO-TOMATO-EGG

IN 1989, a group of American students arrived for a study-abroad year at Yunnan University in Kunming where I was studying. They were from Oberlin College in the US, in search of an authentic Chinese experience, which included having a Chinese roommate. I was one of the lucky students invited to move out of my eight-person college dormitory and live with one American girl named Keely Blanchard. Our room had an en suite bathroom and hot running water. Compared to the queues for the communal bathhouse in the regular dorm, this was heaven.

Every school break, the American students would strap on big backpacks and travel to Dali – it was the place to be. They would return with fascinating photos, snapshots of a place I thought I knew well, but viewed through the lens of an outsider. They marvelled at the otherness of Dali's Bai people, their culture and architecture. Some of the boys would also return with big bags of marijuana to dry out in the dorm room. The weed didn't have much potency, I was told, but they smoked it all the same. What a wacky way to see my hometown, I thought. What are they seeing that I'm not seeing? So I decided to do the same. I saved some money by giving private English lessons and I travelled back to Dali myself that year.

Dali Old Town was tiny back then, just the old walled town and lots of fields around it. I biked to the lake and back; it seemed like such a long journey. Nowadays I run it, and my GPS tells me it's only 5 kilometres each way. To me, the town was grey, like the slate stone of the old city wall.

There were just a few foreign visitors there at the time, and I hung out with the Americans. The only place foreigners were permitted to stay in town was along Huguo Road, in a couple of hotels there, so it was in that area that one or two restaurants had sprung up to serve the backpackers. A guidebook from that era recommends an anonymous restaurant marked only by a Coca-Cola sign:

'Here the prices are right, the portions are huge, and the potato-tomato-egg dish is the best in town. The accommodating hosts are happy to play your cassettes while you dine . . .'

You would be hard-pressed to find an authentic Yunnanese dish named 'potato-tomato-egg', but it caught on among the backpacker set. Over the years, the Coca-Cola restaurant disappeared, but today many new restaurants line every street of Dali Old Town.

In the three decades since Dali was opened to tourists, the town has evolved from a tiny backwater town to a tourism Mecca. Now it is mostly young Chinese travellers who have taken over Dali. A stroll along Renmin Road is proof of that. Boys sit on sidewalks strumming guitars; girls sit nearby and watch, flowers in their hair. Elegantly designed guesthouses, thoughtful craft beer bars and cute, organic cafés sit on every corner. Foreigners are still here, too, but the backpackers are harder to find. The new breed of foreigners in Dali speak Chinese. They study, or own small businesses. Together with Chinese residents who have moved from cities like Beijing and Shanghai, these *xin dali ren* (新大理人), 'new Dali folk', are shaping the city into a sophisticated refuge, distinct from anywhere else in China.

There is a jogging route I like to take from my Dali home. It cuts through the cobbled stones of the Old Town and moves east, bringing me to the lake's edge, which is beautiful in the early morning sunshine. Beside the fields of vegetables and glassy irrigation pools, a whitewashed hacienda-style building comes into view, with a little window opening on to the street. From inside that window come frothy coffees and freshly baked pastries, like a tiny piece of southern Spain in Yunnan.

The eatery is called Green Field Kitchen. The owners, Ms Hong Jiacui and her husband Pan Liangbing are natives of Jiangsu Province, which lies over 2000 kilometres to the east. Hong and her husband came to Dali at the suggestion of her younger brother, Hong Jiaming, who built the first luxury accommodations across the lake in the village of Shuanglang.

'My brother said Dali is interesting, and you can be very creative here, so we came,' Hong explains. She and her husband leased a nearby farm and planted their own vegetables. The produce eventually became too much for them to eat on their own, so two ideas were floated: one, open a farmers' market to sell the produce; and two, start a restaurant.

Just like that, Green Field Kitchen was born, and they hired a Spanish chef, Pedro, to man the paella pan. Pedro first came to China as an engineer, but has since followed his passion to become a chef. I am curious to see how he judges our ham against Spanish Ibérico ham.

I make arrangements with Hong and head over to Green Field Kitchen (翠田). It's gratifying to see how excited Chef Pedro gets when he examines our ham, suggesting a carpaccio, a classic cantaloupe and ham appetiser and a paella. Many of the ingredients will come directly from Green Field Kitchen's own farm.

Under a white canvas canopy beneath an azure sky, we relax with a bottle of Spanish wine while Chef Pedro fusses over the paella in the restaurant's open-air bar. As the table is laid, an old friend of mine, Xi Zhinong, arrives with his younger daughter to complete our lunch party. It's a very Dali gathering: itinerants from all walks of life, dining on Mediterranean dishes using Dali ingredients, with our Bai ham as the star attraction.

Xi is a photographer and Yunnan returnee. He is an outspoken voice for wildlife conservation in China through his photography of Yunnan snub-nosed monkeys. In order to bring his message to a wider audience, he left Yunnan and moved to Beijing in 2002. Then, a few years ago, his older daughter developed issues with her eyesight. The problem became so severe that she had to pause her schooling for a year, so Xi took her back to his childhood home to rediscover its beauty and enjoy the clean mountain air. Her eyesight eventually stabilised, and they decided to move back to Dali for good.

Now Xi is building a nature centre on top of the Cangshan Mountains, and he has a studio in a chic Art Deco building that was once a linen and bedding factory.

Xi's trajectory is not so unusual in Dali. There is a community of thousands of *xin dali ren*, consisting of artists, writers, filmmakers and architects, who left their city lives and relocated to Dali. A visit to the old linen factory reveals lovely cafés and bookshops, interesting photography exhibitions, art and more – proof that Dali's new residents are leaving their mark, moving modern Dali culture forward.

Chef Pedro serves the paella, our ham adorning it like rubies in a crown. Pedro has also made a plate of ham, sliced paper-thin and served raw, with cantaloupe and shavings of aged Parmesan. Chinese people almost never eat ham raw, unlike the Serrano, Ibérico, prosciutto and Parma of continental Europe. But Chef Pedro was confident in our Master's Well ham. 'Why not? It tastes good!' he says.

As ever, food brings people together. We polish off the wine as Dali's sky gets up to its usual tricks – sunshine and spots of rain all at once, four seasons in one day.

CHEF PEDRO'S CHICKEN AND YUNNAN HAM PAELLA

Paella de Pollo y Jamón de Yunnan

SERVES 6–8

---

4 cups ham bone stock (can replace with chicken or vegetable stock)

150g chicken, cut into 1-cm cubes

50g ham, thinly sliced

1½ cups white rice

6 small cherry tomatoes, halved

1 dried chilli pepper

1 cup each of diced green and red bell peppers

1 cup diced red onion

2 cloves of garlic, minced

⅓ cup olive oil

½ cup tomato paste

salt and black pepper, to taste

a few drops of hot chilli sauce

Coat a large paella pan (or flat pan) with olive oil; add chicken and stir fry. Remove 6 pieces and put aside. Add salt, garlic, peppers, onions and hot chilli sauce; sauté for a few minutes.

Add ham slices to pan and stir; remove 6 pieces and put aside. Add tomato paste and salt to taste. Add cherry tomatoes, stir, and remove 6 pieces.

Add rice and mix; add ham bone stock and bring to a boil over high heat, then lower heat and let simmer.

When the liquid has evaporated from the surface of the rice, turn heat to low and cover. Cook for another 5–8 minutes. Be sure to turn the pan now and then to ensure even cooking.

Remove pan from heat, top with reserved chicken, ham and cherry tomatoes. Cover with foil and let sit a few minutes.

Remove cover, garnish with lemon wedges and lettuce. Serve directly from pan, hot or at room temperature.

LIVING NEAR THE ROAD

GIL LIVES in Panqu Village, about 8 kilometres north of Dali Old Town. I had no idea exactly where that was, nor why any *xin dali ren* would be living alone out there. A Joseph Rock wannabe, perhaps? Only a century or so late? Or maybe just another backpacker type hanging out in the country. Whoever he was, my friends in Beijing insisted that I look him up. 'Go visit him, and ask him to cook. You'll see.'

Gil's full name is Gil Gonzalez Foerster, but he was introduced to me as 'Xiaosong', so we spoke Chinese on the phone.

'Just drive past Wuwei Temple, carry on for another three kilometres, then you'll see a white building by the road. Turn left there to come up to my village.'

I turn off the road at the designated white building and continue up through a village toward the slopes of the Cangshan Mountains. With my brother back in Kunming, I am the driver now. At first, the road is well paved, flanked with new houses and parked cars. About a mile further on, it fades into a stone path, eventually narrowing to such a degree that my car cannot go any further. The path winds between stone buildings and beneath bent old trees. The architecture is beautiful, but most houses are unoccupied.

Each metre upward is like going back in time. I peek into yards strangled with the unruly spread of nature. Timber has fallen; stones have split like the segments of an orange. I imagine children playing. I can almost sense cooking smells drifting in the wind like phantoms. This is another one of those ancient villages, mostly abandoned just like Shundang.

'*Ni hao!*' A cheerful voice halts my thoughts. Bounding toward me is the tall, narrow-shouldered figure of Gil, wearing a T-shirt and torn jeans, his grinning face and forearms tanned from the Dali sun. He looks at least ten summers shy of his forty-eight years. 'Come, I'll show you the way to my house,' he says, leading us deeper into the labyrinth of overgrown paths that weave between rough-hewn stone walls.

We arrive at a portion of wall that has collapsed. It is covered with a sheet of plastic. 'My wall fell in,' Gil explains apologetically. 'I'll fix it with stones, but I have to wait until after the rainy season.' Behind this temporary barrier is where Gil has built his life over the past year.

Inside the yard, a section of the concrete courtyard floor has been chipped and peeled away to make space for peppers, beans, kale, wild basil, along with all sorts of herbs.

Beside it, separate from the main house, Gil has constructed a fully fitted kitchen in an old storage shed. The shed boasts three walls and one side of windows, a four-burner stove, an oven and Gil's precious Japanese knives. A neat row of pots, pans and various cooking utensils hang on a metal bar across the back of the kitchen. I look at his shed-kitchen with envy. It is from this space that Gil runs Casa Bai.

'I don't call it a restaurant; it's more like a private dining experience. I cook for friends, special occasions, weddings – small scale, small profile.'

Before he left, Gil was building a reputation in Beijing for another private dining operation, which he ran from his courtyard house. Then he decided to move to Dali where he would have the time and space to make a bigger go of it, all while writing a book on his experiences in China and Asia.

Gil rents the place from a Mr Li, a farmer and retired teacher in his early sixties. Mr Li lived in the house for generations, but has since moved to a modern concrete house closer to the road.

'When I moved in there was no plumbing, and only rudimentary wiring,' Gil tells me. 'The rent is very low because, until a few years ago, local people felt these old houses had no value. I've built a bathroom and installed plumbing, waste water pipes and a septic tank. I've fixed the roof. It's simple, but I like it.'

The main house is a traditional stone, mud and timber affair, and Gil has installed extra windows to brighten up the upper floor where he lives, with guest quarters and a modern bathroom below.

In the yard, Gil shows me multiple varieties of tomatoes. 'My landlord said I was wasting my time, that nothing would grow because this soil hasn't seen the sun for twenty years,' Gil says, motioning to the patch of soil that used to be covered by concrete. 'But this is the second season and already the soil is getting better and better. With all the rain and the sun, you can grow almost anything in Dali.'

What Gil doesn't grow or raise himself he gets from the market on Bo'ai Road in Dali Old Town, cycling the 20 kilometres round trip with a Bai woven basket on his back. 'It's rough on the shoulders when it's full of vegetables,' he grimaces. 'I have to admire how much the old Bai ladies can carry.' I know exactly what he's talking about – Cheng Ayi, my Dali housekeeper, can easily carry a basket that I can barely lift off the floor with both arms.

Next to the tomatoes is a tree producing *xiangyuan* (香橼), a bulbous citrus fruit.

'In the French island of Corsica they call this *cédrat*,' says Gil. 'In English I think it's known as French citron.'

'When I first came to the village, I didn't know what this tree was. But the smell was familiar,' he says. 'It took me a while to connect it to my childhood in France. Now I boil it in sugar, chill, and slice it for a bittersweet after-dinner confectionary. It takes five days to prepare!'

A sprawling web of local flowering vine, *hanjinlian* (旱金莲) or *capucine* in French, has colonised the wall beside the citrus tree. It produces golden yellow flowers that I have seen used in salads in organic, farm-to-table restaurants in California and New Zealand. Gil uses the flowers in his cooking. He uses the leaves, too.

'You know how in Mediterranean or Middle Eastern cooking, people use vine leaves to wrap rice,' says Gil. 'Well, here I use these. I've named the dish *riz en capucine*; I think it's quite poetic.'

These tidbits of cross-cultural culinary information stir up great expectations for the meal to come. We get to work in the open kitchen, beginning by peeling soybeans. I unwrap one of the last remaining chunks of our ham. Just like Chef Pedro, Gil takes the ham, gives it a good sniff, and smiles with satisfaction, eager to make use of what's left. The first of our dishes, he announces in his thick French accent, is *petits pois, carottes et jambon du Yunnan en cocotte*.

'Carrots and peas are simply everywhere in Dali at the moment, and this is a very traditional French way of cooking,' he says. 'The ham lends a nice bit of richness to the dish.' Soon, a rustic stew of stunningly fresh Dali vegetables is married with the salty tang of our ham, the flavour enhanced with garlic, laurel leaf and French thyme.

Baked local mushrooms are next on the menu: *champiñones rellenos con jamon*, stuffed with onions, garlic, parsley and our ham. We then char eggplants from Gil's vegetable patch, which become *caviar d'aubergines*, spiced with lime, chilli and cumin, wrapped in sticky *juanfen* rice sheets (another variety of rice-based pasta, similar to a Vietnamese spring roll wrap) and topped with crushed almonds.

A hearty Spanish tortilla makes use of locally grown zucchini and slices of our ham. Finally, Gil grills traditional *baba* bread from the market and serves it with a handful of peppery greens dressed with olive oil, Chinese vinegar and black garlic.

As we eat in the open air, Gil reflects on the journey that has led him from reporting on social issues in Asia to living in a tumbledown farmhouse in a Bai village, equipped only with a bicycle and woven basket to accomplish his errands.

A Frenchman with a German mother and a French father of Spanish decent,

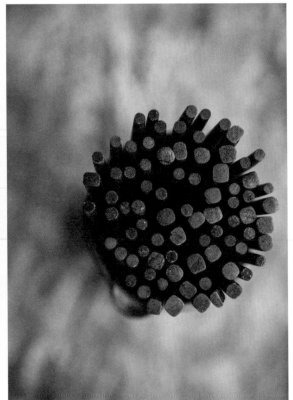

Gil first came to China back in 1996, where he landed an assignment reporting on issues affecting Lijiang's Naxi people.

'I remember taking a fifty-hour train ride from Guangzhou to Kunming,' he tells me. 'It was an amazing experience – back then I couldn't speak a word of Chinese, but I simply fell in love with China. I knew I had to live here.' Since then, Gil has lived on and off in China, moving from Chengdu to Beijing, and now Dali.

As Gil talks, I'm aware that he's moving in the opposite direction of the local people here, and he's not the only one. *Xin dali ren* like Gil are slowly beginning to colonise these isolated, hard-to-reach homes, often for precisely the same reasons their original owners decided to abandon them.

'The pressure is big in the city,' Gil says. 'But here, away from the pollution, people are freer to act on impulse. It's a place where people can invent new lives for themselves.'

Conversation turns to Dali itself, and what makes it special. In his quiet old village house, this is something Gil has had a lot of time to think about. 'In the market in Dali you can buy cigarettes from Myanmar and Vietnam,' he explains. 'You are closer to both those places than to Beijing. In France we call this kind of place *confins*, a border region far from the centre. It's a grey area, lots of trade and people doing things in different ways.' For *xin dali ren*, it's a chance to live a freer life.

'In a place like Dali,' Gil says, 'rules are not so clearly established and people are mixing together more, which makes the place that much more diverse and interesting. This village, for example, is entirely Bai, it's not Han Chinese. It's the opposite of Beijing. These people have never been to Beijing. We are very, very far away. You can feel it.'

I wonder: Does he feel like he is changing the fabric of this place?

'Yes, I admit I'm changing this village, but only in a subtle and limited way. I have good relations with my neighbours. I have some things they don't, like a shower and toilet, but I don't have a car. The changes are small and quiet.'

By the time Gil's lease expires, he'll be in his sixties. Will he still stick around Dali? 'Life is an experiment for me. I've been here one year and I love it. If I feel that one day the experiment is over, I will move on. There is the question of my parents and family getting older, of course. But the words "settle down", I don't really understand them.'

After dinner we take a walk deeper into the old village. We clamber over collapsed walls and rotten timber overgrown with vegetation. Aside from a single light, all the

houses are empty.

We enter one courtyard home, a broken padlock on its gate, the door hanging limply open. Inside, the decorative woodcarving and wall frescos are stunning. It must have been the richest home in the village. Now it's falling apart. It's a treasure, a forgotten relic.

We pick our way back to Casa Bai as the last light of day fades. Much further below, the lights in the concrete homes by the road flicker on, one by one.

TORTILLA DE OTOÑO BY GIL

SERVES 6–8

---

2 medium-sized zucchini, thinly sliced

50g ham, cut into small cubes

1 red bell pepper, diced

1 onion, diced

1 cup fresh mushrooms, diced

1 cup fresh soy beans (edamame) blanched and shelled

½ cup olive oil

Salt and black pepper to taste

5 eggs

Heat 1 tablespoon of oil, toss in ham pieces, cook slightly; add zucchini, sauté zucchini and ham for a few minutes; set aside.

Reheat the leftover oil in the pan and add bell pepper, onion and mushrooms; stir and sauté for 10 minutes. Add soy beans; cook slightly, then set aside.

Beat eggs lightly in a large bowl; add in previously cooked vegetable/ham mix; add salt and pepper to taste.

Using a clean pan, add ¼ cup oil and coat the bottom of the pan evenly. Pour the egg/vegetable mixture into the heated pan, cook on medium heat for 5 minutes until a thin crust forms on the bottom of the pan.

Remove from heat, cover with a large plate; hold the plate tightly over the pan, quickly flipping it upside down to let the tortilla drop on to the plate. Slide the tortilla back into the pan and continue cooking the other side for another 1 to 5 minutes.

Remove and let cool. Before serving, cut into bite-size squares; serve at room temperature with toothpicks in each square.

THREE COURSE TEA:
A BAI WELCOME

AFTER DAYS of high-calorie dining with my ham, I am desperate for a cup of tea. So we call on a local Bai host recommended by one of my WildChina tour guides in Dali. One cannot travel through Dali without attending a three-course tea ceremony, or *san dao cha* (三道茶), a staple at marriages, celebrations and festivals around the lake, or just a formal way to welcome guests.

Our host lives in Zhoucheng, 10 kilometres north of Gil's village. Zhoucheng, together with nearby Xizhou, were among the wealthiest towns along the ancient Tea and Horse Caravan Road. The town has many traditional houses that are well preserved and still in use.

It's not easy to locate an unnumbered house, and we don't have a local guide. We stop by the roadside to ask for directions, which allows us to navigate our way to the last row of houses at the very top of the town. Beyond the house, the gently sloping meadows rise suddenly upwards like a spike on a graph, racing to the 5000-metre-high summit of the Cangshan Mountains.

Upon our arrival, we are led into a lovely courtyard home. Two elderly Bai ladies clothed in beautiful costumes of lilac, blue and black busy themselves with the various stages of the tea ceremony. A pair of tiny metal teapots bubble away on a little brazier of glowing coals, set on the floor of the yard. Traditionally these would have been clay teapots, but metal ones are more durable.

We are invited to sit at a low table on the veranda of the courtyard house. Within minutes, one of the Bai ladies emerges from the kitchen with three cups and a kettle. The teacups are small, similar in size to a shot glass, and a lot nicer than the paper cups we've been receiving everywhere else.

The three courses of tea taste rather un-Chinese. Chinese people tend to drink tea unadorned by milk, sugar or spices. But here the tea is flavoured with Sichuan peppercorns and cinnamon. I have a sudden craving for a splash of milk and sugar to make Indian chai. Even during the tea ceremony, one can feel Dali is removed from the rest of China. Of course, further along the Tea and Horse Caravan Road, tea traditions change again. In Tibet, tea is brewed and poured into a special bamboo churn. From there it is churned vigorously with a chunk of yak butter and a little salt (maybe from Master's Well Village) before being served in a bowl.

We proceed through the three courses of tea, changing for a fresh set of cups after each course. Teacups in hand, we mill around the courtyard, watching the furiously shifting clouds atop the peaks of the Cangshan Mountains.

THREE COURSE TEA

COURSE 1: BITTER TEA, OR *KU CHA* (苦茶) The tea leaves used for the first course are roasted in a small locally-made clay jar. A dying charcoal fire works best for roasting them. Toss 2 teaspoonfuls of green tea leaves together with 1 teaspoonful of rice in the small jar; hold the jar by its handle, roast a few seconds, remove and shake to even out the heat exposure. Change direction, roast again, and repeat a few more times until a fragrant and nutty scent rises in light smoke from the jar. Pay close attention so as not to burn the leaves.

Now pour 1 cup of boiling water into the jar, let sit for two minutes, and pour into small teacups to serve.

It's slightly bitter, with a dry, toasty finish.

COURSE 2: SWEET TEA, OR *TIAN CHA* (甜茶) The second course is similar to a sweet ginger 'tea' – a mixture of ginger and brown sugar and no tea leaves. The ginger tea base has been sitting by a charcoal fire for two hours when we arrive, and is ready for use any time.

With this course, one of the Bai ladies brings out some *rushan*, a paper-thin sheet of local cheese, and roasts it lightly on the charcoal. She then dices it finely with a knife.

She adds a teaspoon of roasted sesame seeds and a teaspoon of the diced *rushan* into a small teacup. She pours in the ginger tea over the cheese and sesame and then serves.

It's an intriguing combination with a rich, sweet finish.

COURSE 3: LINGERING TEA, OR *HUIWEI CHA* (回味茶) This final round of tea, as with the previous course, uses no tea leaves at all. Instead, it uses mouth-numbing Sichuan pepper and dried chilli. Roast two whole pieces of dried chilli, add a few pieces of Sichuan pepper to 3 cups of water and simmer for an hour or two. Add 1 tablespoon of honey to the cup before serving.

Our host emphasised again and again that it takes a lot of skill to get just the right flavour. If there is too much of one ingredient, the tea will be too spicy; if there is too little, there will be no flavour. If you simmer the tea over an electric burner, it's a different flavour from tea simmered over charcoal. A great deal of skill and practice is involved, but the result is a tiny cup of sweet, fiery goodness that gets the appetite going.

DALI SOUL FOOD

ON THE last day of our trip, Cheng Ayi invites us over for lunch. Cheng Ayi is the housekeeper at my Dali house, just inside the south gate of the old city. She works there when guests are staying and keeps an eye on it for the rest of the year. *Ayi* literally means aunt (specifically a sister of the mother), but it is also used to describe female domestic workers, or simply as a term of address like 'auntie', which people – especially children – use to address women a generation older than themselves.

I first met Cheng Ayi a few years back at a Dali guesthouse I was staying in while my own house was being renovated. The guesthouse had a lovely, lush garden with stone tables and chairs for tea. My kids were eager to spend every minute playing in the garden, and one of their favourite activities was helping Cheng Ayi, then a member of the hotel staff, to sweep the garden and feed stray kittens. I couldn't peel my girls away from her, so I knew she was the perfect 'child whisperer' to hire. When the guesthouse later closed for renovations, I offered her a job.

Cheng Ayi lives in a Bai village fifteen minutes from the old town by bicycle, halfway to the lakeshore. The east wall of her yard is the village's last solid structure before it gives way to emerald-green fields. Further east of her house, a raised concrete path winds through beds of potatoes, fava beans, lettuce and rice, depending on the season. Marijuana plants grow like weeds in lazy clumps. Farmers park their bicycles along the path and clamber down to tend the produce on this fertile land, watered constantly by trickling streams rolling down from the Cangshan Mountains.

In Cheng Ayi's yard, a persimmon tree is just beginning to blossom, its flowers hanging down like little bells. We are not the only guests; whenever neighbours or friends turn up randomly, they, too, are invited to eat. But now it is approaching noon and there is no food to be seen. Nobody is in the kitchen. Instead, Cheng Ayi and a neighbour are out lighting a fire on a patch of earth.

This, I soon learn, is because she prefers to cook this particular dish in the open air, freeing up the kitchen for other dishes. The dish is called *luoguo men fan*, a one-pot hodgepodge of rice with potatoes or beans (or whatever is on hand), together with a little meat – in this case, our ham.

Once the fire is crackling, Cheng Ayi simmers some rice in a cauldron-like black pot. I watch as she drops in chunks of yellow-fleshed potato – supplied by a passing neighbour moments before – and chopped pieces of our ham. 'It should cook for twenty to thirty minutes, and the important thing is, once the water has evaporated and you can see rice on the surface, you mustn't stir it anymore. If you continue to stir the rice, it turns into mush,' she says. This sounds the same as what Chef Pedro has told me about his paella.

Like much of the rural village cooking we've experienced, Cheng Ayi's recipes are a blend of instinct and experience.

'It take years of practice not to burn the rice when you cook over a fire like this,' says Cheng Ayi proudly as she lifts the heavy pot and turns it on the flames. Every few minutes she adjusts the pot's angle without ever opening it to stir or check inside. I wonder how she's not burning her hands. Cheng Ayi looks at me and exclaims, 'I got this pot when my son was only six!' Her son is now a married man. In fact, through the door of the kitchen, his wife is frying slices of goat cheese in a wok, browning them one piece at a time and then removing them from the heat with chopsticks.

Cheng Ayi's son was married a month ago during Chinese New Year. Her daughter-in-law is a Yi woman from Weishan, which Cheng Ayi doesn't mind. The most important thing is for her son to get married and start having children. 'Want to see her Yi wedding dress and shoes?' She momentarily abandons the rice pot to rush into the newly renovated quarter of the house. She points out the elaborate embroidery and bright colours of the dress. 'Her mother started working on this when she was a little girl,' Cheng Ayi says, 'stitch by stitch. It's very important that Yi girls are married with beautiful wedding dresses.'

Cheng Ayi's joy at her new status as a mother-in-law infuses her entire home. She lost her husband to illness when her boy was just a few years old, and her son's marriage signals a generational shift. Now she's a matriarch, no longer just a widow. And she's soon to reign over the household, once her first grandchild is born. In the mean time, she spared no expense renovating the house and hosting a big wedding banquet.

Smoke from the small fire drifts upward. Cheng Ayi's daughter-in-law picks some mint to make a simple salad. More neighbours drop by just to say hello, or to offer advice on the turning of the pot or the readiness of the rice, or to contribute another handful of vegetables. 'Everybody leaves their doors open around here,' says Cheng Ayi.

Then the moment of truth: Cheng Ayi lifts the charred lid from the pot. Once the rush of steam clears, we see that the water has all departed, leaving behind

brilliant white rice, perfectly fluffy, studded with pink, fleshy ham and rich yellow potato. It's perfect.

A table – or rather, a big plank of wood – is propped up under the persimmon tree, with the rice taking centre stage. The daughter-in-law's strips of fried cheese are spiced with a dusting of chilli, Sichuan pepper and salt. She has also made a mint salad dressed simply with a little soy sauce, dark vinegar, salt and pepper, just like at A Herd of Goats. One more dish, a stir-fry of local celery, green peppers and julienned strips of pork, completes the spread. Colour, texture, presentation – it's a beautiful collection of food.

We eat together under some shade in the midday heat. Our ham is once again the star; its smoky, fatty, salty essence has leeched into the pot, gently flavouring the rice and potatoes. Cheng Ayi is in her element, telling us stories of her time as a construction worker, which is when she mastered the art of lighting fires outdoors. 'I can even light them in the rain!' she laughs.

She eats three bowls of the hammy rice before dashing away to get her *cao mao* – her straw hat – for a portrait photo with Liz. 'I'm so happy today!' she tells me. I think I know how she feels, It's a contentment like no other when everything comes together – food, family, friends and neighbours – so naturally. '*Ziran lai, ziran lai*', as Madame Chen would say.

CHENG AYI'S ONE-POT HAM AND RICE

洋芋火腿锣锅焖饭

SERVES 6–8

---

4 cups rice, rinsed

4 cups water

500g potatoes, peeled and cut into 2cm cubes

250g ham with some fat, cut into 2cm chunks

Pour rice, potato and ham into a pot; add water, cover with lid, and bring to boil. Lower the heat and simmer for 15 minutes with the lid on.

Rotate pot every minute or two for even heating, continuing for about 10 minutes. Make sure not to stir the rice while cooking. When the steam coming out from the pot is fragrant with the aroma of the ham, it is done.

Serve hot, warm or at room temperature.

Note: Potato can be replaced with fava beans or string beans if desired.

EPILOGUE

LIZ AND Tom have flown back to Beijing, back to their day jobs. All alone in my Dali house, I make a cup of roasted green tea and carry it up to the terrace. As I turn on my computer and prepare to write, I wonder:

What does this journey mean to me?

More than anything, I think it confirms that I never left this place in spirit. I was in Dali for only the first ten years of my life, and it was a life of poverty, hardship and sometimes sadness. Yet being here again anchors me. The light blue expanse of Erhai Lake to the east, and the dark green wall of the Cangshan Mountains to the west, cradle me as if I were still a baby. I take in the aroma of pink camellias: the scent of home. I take a sip of the green tea: the taste of home.

But it's not just the sensory messages of Dali that feel like home. It's the way people are to one another. The idea that 'your business is my business', and the way Zhang Jiahong handles every single one of our meals in Yunlong, and goes the extra mile to find me the perfect leg of ham. It's the way Cheng Ayi lives with an open door policy, inviting everyone who passes by in for lunch. It's the way the wedding couple welcomes me, a stranger, to join their celebration. Everything is informal, but people go out of their way to make you feel like you are among family.

Another essential part of Dali is the way people confide in you. Dali folk don't build fences around themselves; they take me as a member of their tribe. I feel it in the way Shi Fumei quietly tells me about her grinding daily routine, not complaining, but with a hint of a wish for a break; the way Chef Qian stares out through his cigarette smoke and talks about his dream to visit the mountain people. This makes me feel that they are my people. They tell me exactly how much money they make selling goats, pickles or a pair of shoes. They tell me about problems at their children's school or about their grandparent's health. It's not because of anything I do; it's simply the way Dali people are.

I reflect back on the places we visited. Master's Well Village, brimming with life. Fragile Shaxi, on course to becoming the next tourist hot spot. Weishan, plotting its future as the food capital of Yunnan. Each place is charting its own course, for better or worse. Yet somehow, the Bai, Yi, Hui and Han – we all carry on. The culture goes deep; no matter how much money there is to be made, the shops will always close for Chinese New Year, festivals, weddings and funerals.

So I try not to worry about the impact of tourism. Change is inevitable. All we can do is to try to shepherd it, to celebrate authenticity and quality wherever we find it. After all, Dali survived the Mongols, it survived the Han, it even survived the backpackers. It's still Bai, and I have a feeling it always will be.

I hope the age-old traditions will endure. Salt-making, ham-curing, basket-weaving, three-course tea, folk singing and more. As long as people appreciate the beauty and value of these traditions, we have reason to hope that they are here to stay.

That's probably my most important reason for writing this book.

I have been in the travel industry for sixteen years now, and I am still no expert at issuing airline tickets. Why do I stay in this business? Because I love the people and the small experiences that we encounter while travelling. It's not a five-star hotel or a white sandy beach that define a place for me; it's the taste of a chicken curry, the scent of jasmine, the simple story of a doorman who worked at the same hotel for seventy years. These details capture the beauty of travel in stunning definition.

I observe China, and particularly Yunnan, in this heightened form every day, and it compels me to share the beauty with everyone who wishes to experience it. China is not just red lanterns and rickshaws, not just Yangtze River cruises and bicycles, not just smoggy factories. China has so much more to offer. There's the breathtaking starry nights in the mountains of Yunnan, the meticulously farmed fields around Dali, and the unadorned hospitality of everyone in this book and many others like them. All it takes is stepping off the tourist circuit to discover the wilder China that lies just a little further from the road.

Eventually it's time to pack. I pull out a folded duffle bag and set about packing the goodies I've bought on the road in Dali: a beautiful wooden chopping board from a market in Yunlong; an enamel washbasin with a 'happiness' character and two birds printed on it; a roll of hemp string and funeral papers that I plan to use as gift wrap; bags and bags of Weishan pickles; and two perfect white cylinders of Master's Well salt. I look at all the items fondly. It's strange what we do, hoping that souvenirs will somehow safeguard and preserve our memories for us. In the end, it's the stories, images and flavours that remain.

Once I'm packed, there's time for one more meal. I'm alone in my house, so I go downstairs to the kitchen and cook a dish of fried rice with ham. It's a simple, one-pot meal that my dad taught me to make when I was 10. I make a mental note to teach my own children the next chance I get.

FRIED RICE WITH HAM AND EGGS

火腿蛋炒饭

SERVES 4–6

---

4 eggs

a pinch of *caoguo* (optional)

½ cup canola oil

400g lean ham, skinned, cut into thin pieces

2 dried chilli peppers, whole or cut into 3cm pieces for stronger flavour (optional)

6 cups cooked white rice

1-2 twigs of spring onion, finely chopped, about ½ cup when loosely packed

salt, to taste (optional)

Break the eggs into a bowl, mix in a pinch of *caoguo*, beat with a pair of chopsticks until yolks break and mix with the whites; set aside.

Heat oil in a wok or frying pan over high heat. To see if the oil is hot, use chopsticks to drop in a bit of beaten egg; if oil bubbles around the egg, it's ready. When ready, pour in all the beaten egg, letting it spread out and bubble up. Use a spatula to break into bite-size pieces. Place into a bowl for later use. Drain oil back into wok.

Use remaining oil, still over high heat, to fry ham and dried chilli pepper for 30 seconds. When ham starts to brown, add the eggs back in. Stir and turn a few times. Then add rice, stirring a few times. Turn the heat to medium and cook for a few minutes to thoroughly heat the rice; add a tablespoon of water if the rice is too dry.

Taste before adding more salt. Usually ham is sufficiently salty for this dish. Add half the chopped spring onion, saving the other half for garnish. Turn rice mixture a few more times. Place into a large bowl, sprinkle remaining spring onion on top. Serve hot or at room temperature.

AFTERWORD

IT'S BEEN more than a year since this project began, so I called around
to see what, if anything, had changed in the lives of the people I got to
know on my trip. Some have continued along much the same as before,
while others have gone through major life changes.

The Yunlong area as a whole has suffered the most. Salt Maker
Yang Zhiguang isn't selling much salt, so he is dabbling in construction
material trading and the local veterinarian business.

Farmer Yang Xuegong, our ham curer, was raising chickens when
his chickens got sick. So he now focuses on selling baby chicks, which
brings to mind those delicious eggs I ate in the open air of his yard.
One of his sons ended up leaving home to work as a labourer in another
part of Yunnan for extra income. He and his wife remain optimistic that
business will turn around.

Zhang Jiahong, our local fixer in Yunlong, continues his habit of
directing the lives of those around him. He tells me that he's offered
the salt maker a piece of business advice: stay focused on making the
best, most hygienic, highest quality salt. I am not sure whether the salt
maker will heed that advice. Sadly, Zhang's right-hand man, the one he
rescued from alcoholism at A Herd of Goats, was diagnosed with cancer
and is refusing chemotherapy. Zhang, as usual, stays hopeful that some
local herbal brew might work.

On a brighter note, Zhang is organising some farmers to do organic
farming. 'We have the best red rice in one village, and a special type
of skinned ham in another. I am thinking of signing these farmers up
to produce organically, with no pesticides or animal feeds, and I'll run
the distribution. Just like in Japan, one village, one product – develop
expertise!' I couldn't agree with him more, and I wish him success.

Over in Jianchuan County, new county leadership developed the
Thirteenth Five-Year Plan, which contains blueprints for a circular
tourist route that links Jianchuan Old Town, Shaxi, the Shibaoshan

Grottoes, Stone Dragon Bai Village, a nearby Yi village and another salt well along the ancient trading route. They are launching a joint promotion campaign for of all these sites to boost tourism.

Chief Li, the Folk Song King, believes this new development plan will help promote folk songs as well as tourism. He is happy with his current class of twenty-three musical disciples. And with the increasing number of local restaurants and guesthouses, he is more in demand than ever to perform at dinners and events. His family life stays the same, though he didn't say much to me on that subject. I wonder if I should have asked him to sing the answers to me?

Shi Fumei is impossible to reach on the phone, but her niece in Kunming relayed a message to me that everyone at home is doing well, as is her son at university in Xi'an. Grandpa troops along, too. They are now renovating part of the house, installing new roof tiles. That doesn't surprise me; Mrs Shi would never tolerate a leaky roof.

Jacques Feiner is now Head of General Planning for the Swiss region of Graubünden, also called Canton of Grisons. He tells me, 'Mountain people somehow always have to get back to their roots.' I'm glad he is there. His Chinese counterpart, Huang Yingwu, just successfully raised 3 million *yuan* through crowd-sourcing via WeChat, a Chinese social media platform. His experiment with community-based conservation efforts was featured in a *New York Times* article.

In Xiaguan, Uncle Yang and his wife happily continue their routine. When I talked to him, the fava beans and garlic scapes were coming in, and once again the cherries were about twenty days away. I always seem to just miss them. His wife tells me the glucosamine pills have helped her knees and she's travelling more, but so far only to domestic destinations. Uncle Yang plays chess and goes fishing from time to time.

In Weishan, Madame Chen is now 80 and still pickling. All four of her children are in the family business. The eldest son retired from his government job in 2015 and is now heading up pickle production. 'Business continues to grow,' said son number two.

Chef Qian has renovated the backyard of his restaurant 'according to traditional style,' he emphasised. I inquired whether the renovation of Weishan's scorched tower has been completed. 'Yes, finished last

October,' he tells me. That was fast. Are people happy with the renovation work? 'Well, it's satisfactory, but you can't replace the old with the new,' he says.

In Dali Old Town, Hong Jiacui, the owner of Green Field Kitchen, now runs a successful local farmers' market, Chai Mi Duo (柴米多) (which means 'plentiful firewood and rice'), and they have also opened another restaurant inside the old town, named Chai Mi Duo Restaurant. The new restaurant features Spanish and other fusion dishes using produce from their organic farm.

Xi Zhinong, my photographer friend, unveiled his nature centre on the top of the Cangshan Mountains in the spring of 2016.

Gil still lives in Dali, successfully running his home food experience while writing his book.

The Person of the Year award ought to go to Cheng Ayi, who just became a grandmother. The baby boy had not yet been named when I called.

As for myself, since returning to Beijing, I set up a new e-commerce sharing website to connect Chinese travellers with local hosts like Cheng Ayi and Gil all around China. The website is www.newugo.com.

I have also realised how much I cherished the moments I shared with each person in this book. They are just ordinary citizens, yet they are the ones who define Dali and Yunnan for me. They are the ones who carry on the traditions that came to us through hundreds of years of heritage.

They are the ones who make Dali what it is, which, for me, is home.

BIBLIOGRAPHY

Davidson, Alan, *The Oxford Companion to Food (2nd Edition)*, Oxford: Oxford University Press, 2006.

Fitzgerald, C. P., *The Tower of Five Glories: A study of the Min Chia of Ta Li, Yunnan,* Hong Kong: Caravan Press, 2005 (first published 1941).

Fuchs, Jeff, *The Ancient Tea Horse Road: Travels with the Last of the Himalayan Muleteers*, Ottawa: Renouf Pub Co Ltd, 2008.

Goodman, Jim, *Yunnan: China South of the Clouds*, Hong Kong: Odyssey Books & Maps, 2009.

Hosie, Alexander, *Three Years in Western China: Narrative of Three Journeys in Ssu-ch'uan, Keui-chow and Yun-nan*, Whitefish, Montana: Kessinger Publishing, 2008 (first published 1890).

Huang Yinwu, *Reading Time in Shaxi*, Kunming: The Nationalities Publishing House of Yunnan, 2009.

IRL – Institute ETH On Behalf of SDC Jianchuan County Government, 'The Shaxi Rehabilitation Project, Building a Future for the Past Along the Ancient Tea and Horse Caravan Trail'.

Kingdon-Ward, Francis, *Through Western Yunnan* (downloaded via Project Guttenberg, no identifiable publisher), 1922.

Kurlansky, Mark, *Salt: A World History*, New York: Penguin Books, 2003.

Morrison, George Ernest, *An Australian in China: The Narrative of a Quiet Journey Across China to Burma,* (downloaded via Project

Guttenberg, no identifiable publisher), 1895.

'The Mud Fish Song', in Zhang Wen, Chen Ruihong, *Shibaoshan Chuantong Baiqu Jijing* (Collection of Shibaoshan Traditional Bai Tunes), Kunming: The Nationalities Publishing House of Yunnan, 2005,[independently translated for this book by Zhang Mei].

Qian Changgui, Chen Xikui, *Yunlong County Almanac*, Beijing: China Agriculture Press, 1992.

ACKNOWLEDGEMENTS

I STARTED out not knowing what this book would turn out to be. Nevertheless, I had a hunch we were on the right path because the process was filled with laughter and fun. I couldn't have done this without my core team. The trip with photographer Elizabeth Phung, creative director Thomas O'Malley, and my younger brother Zhang Ye doubling as our driver, ranks among the best journeys in my life.

At every meal, Liz climbed on to tabletops to capture the perfect shot. Liz taught me a fresh perspective to appreciate the details and beauty in life.

Tom urged me to travel deeper into the country to find the source of our ham, and generally encouraged me to push boundaries. He also worked with me tirelessly to refine the concept and zoom in on individual stories. Tom, thank you for not being afraid to tell me 'it's a wet fart' when it really is. This book wouldn't have been possible without you.

My brother often drove through the night while the rest of us dozed off. He was quiet, but always there to support me. When we forgot the salt in Master's Well Village, he walked back up the mountain to retrieve it. Thank you for your never-ending love and support.

Lisa Schwartz always understands me. When I came up with the idea of the book to showcase local experiences, Lisa was the first person I went to for advice. Thank you for encouraging me to pursue the idea and for taking the time to help me refine it.

Mr Yang Huiming, the Director of the Bureau of Culture in Shaxi, was away from home when we came to Shaxi, but his presence was felt every minute. He worked his phone remotely and introduced us to Chief Li, Shi Fumei and the young couple getting married. He also took me on a long hike from Shaxi to Lijiang more than a decade ago. Thank you for making Shaxi so dear to me.

Mr Chen Weigang, WildChina's local partner in Dali, directed me to the three-course-tea maker and helped with logistics.

Mr Long Chunlin, a famed botanist from Yunnan, helped me with the plant names.

Christiana Zhu, the Marketing Director for WildChina, supported me enthusiastically throughout this project. Without Chris, I would have missed all the deadlines. Thank you, Chris, for believing in me, and for presenting the draft to Penguin.

To the WildChina team with Bao Xun at the helm: Thank you for holding down the fort while I laboured away in front of a computer. The team's dedication to helping travellers gain access to authentic China inspires me to write about the local experiences that make China and Yunnan so special.

To the NewUGo team: Thank you for validating my belief that local travel experiences like those documented in this book are of value. Thank you for believing in me.

To Fuchsia Dunlop, absolutely the best cookbook writer on Chinese cuisine of our time: I am deeply honoured that you agreed to read my recipes and tell me when things were confusing. Thank you for your help and expertise.

Of course, thanks go to Imogen Liu and her many talented colleagues at Penguin Random House. Thank you for believing in me and working with me tirelessly to restructure the chapters, refine the tone and find illustrators/designers to change the letters into beautiful pieces of art. Imogen's editing, always thoughtful and light, never steered me wrong.

Caryn Schwartz, working behind the scenes, took on the tedious task of line editing and making sense of my words.

Suo Di, the talented Penguin designer, tolerated my never-ending changes.

Jason Pym, whose wonderfully illustrated map still adorns the wall of my dining room in Dali, took the time to draw the illustrations for this book. His passion and knowledge of Dali shine through in his simple drawings of the region.

My family provided the foundation for me to write this book. My father, Zhang Minqiang, tirelessly answered my questions about all things Yunnan; my aunt, Zhang Xinxian, the best cook in the Zhang family, inspired me with the best Yunnan food. My other aunt, Zhang

Jixian, gave me the pickle recipe; my uncle, Zhang Jianping, introduced me to the food culture of Weishan.

My three children make Dali special for me. They were the first ones to notice the holler of '*Mae feng mi!*' (honey for sale!) in the streets of Dali. They tolerated my endless travels and inspired me to keep telling the stories of Yunnan. Thank you for the wonderful hugs and kisses that keep me going.

There is also one gentleman from Thailand to whom I am indebted beyond words, Khun Sirin Nimmanhaeminda. Khun Sirin, then President of Krung Thai Bank of Thailand gave me the scholarship to attend Harvard Business School in 1994 when I was making a monthly salary of twenty dollars. He opened the door for me to see the world and told me that he was doing it as a gift to Yunnan. I also want to thank Minister Tarrin Nimmanhaeminda, Khun Suwit Udomsab, Mr Zhao Songyu, Mrs Guo Yuhua, Mr Du Jianan, Mr Li Chao who helped turn the scholarship into reality without the opportunity to leave Yunnan, I would not have been able to see the beauty of Yunnan with such clarity.

Last but not the least is my husband, John E. Pomfret. Thank you for giving me the courage to write. Thank you for appreciating my 'sappiness'. Thank you for taking the time to help with editing, cutting out the many instances of 'contentedly' and 'lovely'. You taught me how to write. I still remember, while we were driving toward Master's Well Village in 2015, I realised that I had planned the trip without taking John's birthday into account. I panicked, and called to offer a 'happy birthday' greeting. John laughed and told me, 'Just chill, have a good trip and come home.' Thank you for being so tolerant of my travels to make WildChina possible, and to make this book possible. And thank you for giving me a warm, welcoming home I can always return to.

Zhang Mei
27 March, 2016

INDEX

PENGUIN BOOKS

UK | USA | Canada | Ireland | Australia
India | New Zealand | South Africa | China

Penguin Books is part of the Penguin Random House group of companies
whose addresses can be found at global.penguinrandomhouse.com.

Penguin
Random House
PENGUIN BOOKS CHINA

First published by Penguin Group (Australia)
in association with Penguin (Beijing) Ltd, 2016

1 3 5 7 9 10 8 6 4 2

Text copyright © Zhang Mei, 2016

Book design by Di Suo © Penguin Group (Australia)
Photography © Elizabeth Phung
Illustrations by Jason Pym © Penguin Group (Australia)
Printed and bound in China by RR Donnelley Asia Printing Solutions Ltd.

National Library of Australia
Cataloguing-in-Publication data:

Zhang, Mei,
Travels through Dali : with a leg of ham / Mei Zhang.
9780734399427 (hardback)
Dali Xian (China)–Description and travel–Social life and customs.

915.135

penguin.com.cn